Voice of the Borderlands

Voice OF THE Borderlands

DRUM HADLEY

Foreword by GARY SNYDER
Illustrations by ANDREW RUSH

RIO NUEVO PUBLISHERS
TUCSON, ARIZONA

RIO NUEVO PUBLISHERS®

P.O. Box 5250, Tucson, Arizona 85703-0250

(520) 623-9558, www.rionuevo.com

Library of Congress Cataloging-in-Publication Data

Hadley, Drummond.
The voice of the Borderlands / by Drum Hadley ; foreword by Gary Snyder ;
illustrations by Andrew Rush.
    p. cm.
Includes index.
ISBN-13: 978-1-887896-83-2
ISBN-10: 1-887896-83-X
1. Mexican American Border Region--Poetry. 2. Ranch life--Poetry. I.
Title.
PS3558.A318V65 2005
811'.54--dc22

                    2005009645

Design: Karen Schober, Seattle, Washington

Printed on 100% postconsumer recycled paper. Printed in Canada.

10   9   8   7   6   5   4   3   2   1

For the hands of my mother,
Puddie Hadley, who gave me her
love for the land.

· · · · ·

These poems record voices and events occurring over decades of life in the Borderlands
or in places that have affected the Borderlands. The italicized names beneath poems may
represent a voice captured, a story's main subject, or, in many cases, its inspiration.
Some names and places have been changed out of respect for the memories of the dead
or for the sensitivities of the living.

—DRUM HADLEY

I take SPACE to be the central fact to man

born in America, from Folsom cave to now.

— CHARLES OLSON

Table of Contents

Foreword

I first heard Drum Hadley read poems and tell stories of his life in the Southwest many years ago. I knew right then that he had a unique gift of both speaking and hearing. That, combined with an actual working practice on ranches, working cattle, handling horses, gave him his path. We were all practicing the lessons learned from our somewhat older elders: Charles Olson, Robert Duncan, Kenneth Rexroth, and more. Drum's particular landscape, labor, and skill were neither Californian nor East Coast urban, he always stayed prickly dusty southwest, and with a hat. We admired his power of language, his economy, and also his absolute courage to be who he was and break whatever rules of modernist poetry he felt like, including being sentimental about women, dogs, and horses.

One time Drum and I walked miles through the ocotillo and cardon of the Pinacate desert in Sonora, finding our way back to the truck by compass. I once battered my body almost to surrender trying to keep on a horse when they were moving cattle along the steep brushy walls of his canyons. I helped him act up with his reata at a poetry reading in Kentucky. Over the years his collection grew, and time after time we urged him to go ahead and get it into print. He was never quite satisfied and always writing more. Cowboy poet? These are poems and anecdotes and little mini oral histories of actual ranching such as you rarely hear in the ballad-meter camp.

So I'm finally seeing, in this generous collection finally out, what Drum's about. A lot of it has to do with a way of knowing, and an understated teaching of self-sufficiency, and the surprisingly deep possibilities of observation. Plus a voice of song—Drum's own ear for music and a play between boney stoic hardiness and genuinely sweet love and acceptance of huge landscape and impermanence.

The voice is not just Drum's, it is those words and anecdotes of countless working men and a few women—many of whom were his immediate teachers and neighbors over the years. Real people, who are a bit intimidated by what's in books, who talk story and drink coffee, who joke while they work. Some speak Spanish, and Drum's expert at that, too. Drum steps into narratives and territories that no one else out West much speaks of, like the drug culture of *vaquero* smugglers along the miles of desert mountain borders; or the business lunches and board rooms of Wall Street and midtown Manhattan where people try to buy ranches. Drum Hadley is in fact both the rich rancher of some of his poems, and the saddle-weary youth riding the far wing of a Mexican roundup. He's also (though nothing of it in the book) the innovative leader of a huge-scale ecological transformation of ranching, the Animas Foundation.

There's a lot here that's painful and not correct, let's learn from it. The best outcome, in these poems, for any of us is what the old Chinese poets used to say: "Going back to the mountains and rivers from whence we came." Tough message? But still—love poems.

—GARY SNYDER
KITKITDIZZE
FEBRUARY 2005

Preface—The Oral Tradition

In the early 1960s I left academia and got a job as a cowboy in the Southwestern Borderlands. I took these as given, as I do now: that we are created in the image of the Earth, and that we become what surrounds us. I wanted to explore the possibility that the language used by cowboys and *vaqueros* would reflect some essence of the rough mountains, mesas, and arroyos of the Sonoran and Chihuahuan Deserts in which they worked cattle and horses. I imagined that words might have an other-than-intellectual origin and understanding, that they might be rather of the body's blood, the sweat and tears of loss and acceptance.

I was not interested in the definitions of academic folklorists, nor in the oral cowboy poetry tradition presently defined by rhyme schemes, but in the true poetic language, insight, and raw vitality that exist in the unself-conscious stories, sayings, songs, and humorous tales of rangeland cowboys. I *was* interested in the possibility of an imagery and sound not written primarily for other poets, fine as that carpentry may be, but written for anyone with eyes to see or the ear to listen.

When I worked as a *vaquero,* and later as a rancher, I was forced to listen in a new way to hear what I needed to learn, to hear poetry wherever it was. Of course this way of listening and the poetry it found are not at all limited to the *vaquero*-cowboy culture. Each trade, each people have their own language and a poetry that naturally emerges.

Listening to these Southwestern story traditions and oral frontier histories, trying to translate the trade of the cowboy with its particular use of language and imagery without losing the natural music and rhythmic flow of the words as they were spoken, has been a long bronc ride through a rocky but beautiful canyon.

When I cowboyed in Mexico in the late 1960s, it was evident that the *vaqueros* were part of a cowboy tradition that had disappeared shortly after the turn of the century in this country except in a few of the most isolated rangelands. There are several difficulties a sophisticated reader might encounter in reading the language of the *vaqueros* and cowboys. Not only is it a dialect in sound, but also it transmits an archetypal, mythological sense that is in direct contrast to what has come to be the trend of mainstream thinking in America. The knowledge and existence that the cowboy culture contains are as strange as a foreign language to the minds of city people used to the verticalities of modern life: flashing lights, quick moving cars, and truncated language and thought.

Among cowboys the prefix "old" is almost always used when referring to another person. It is a term of respect, usually adding presence to the person referred to. Of course, because it has to do with time, its use also involves an increased consciousness of beginning and end.

I have not altered language cadences that might seem repetitive. They are repetitive, as a chant is, as the throbbing of the heart is, as the sun coming up and setting each day. They are knowingly repetitive as an old cowboy who sits on his wood porch, who watches the sun set, and the stars appear, and the moon move across the evening, who gets up, stretches, and says, "Well, guess it's time to go to bed again."

BOOK ONE

· · · · ·

Cowboys
and
Horses

· · · · ·

PREAMBLE

Now come hear these rough rhymes sing
Like sunlight on the ridgelines of far mountain ranges,
Range upon range of recognition in the dawn.
This book documents the settling of the Borderlands.
It is a weaving of humor and tears,
Of men and women grounded in the earth,
The livelihoods and folk knowledges,
The wisdoms fast disappearing,
The horses, the cowboys, the beautiful lands.
It is heard across these howling distances,
Of faraway mountain ranges,
Voices echoing across cedar breaks, arroyos, and mesas.
As far as the eye can see, the distances cling to each spoken word
As each word clings to the distances and tries to take them in.
But if you listen, you can still hear them
When you read these words slowly by the fire
And your voice becomes the people,
The lions, the wildlife, and the land.

• • • • •

Whoosh   Whoosh

"*El veintiocho de noviembre presente lo tengo yo,*
Que en el rancho Los Chirriones la corrida comenzó."
Swish, swish, swish,
The sound of the wind in the grama grasses ...

Prayer for the Land

Old Earth

We are gathering these Borderlands together,
Mesas, arroyos, and valleys as far as our eyes can see,
Blue mountain range upon mountain range forever,
Turning towards dawnlight, then into the evening West,
As far as pale North sky circling South, to where *vaqueros*
Come crossing horseback by the broken mesas in Mexico.
There's a low light stretching from the sea of undulating cloud,
Sky streaked down to touch Earth from Heaven.
Who are you who cross through that dusk light before us?
Past old-growth juniper, cedar, and mescal,
Across this great sea of sky, Old Singer,
We hear your voice calling,
"Turn back towards me, come back to Earth."

Turquoise Stones

Before Dawn

Rain is falling on the leaves.
In the soft lamplight we wait.
Soon, it will be time to saddle up and go,
But, listen again to the rain on the leaves.

When You're a Cowboy

When you go riding into the dawnlight each morning,
When you're riding for a lifetime,
First you have to take care of your horse.
You've got to brush his back,
And make sure no burrs
Have gotten stuck under the saddle blanket,
And check his tail for cockleburs too.
Then you've got to brush his chest, where the breast collar goes,
And under his belly,
Where the forward cinch and the flank cinch go.
Then you throw the saddle blankets onto his back,
And the saddle on top of the blankets.
Then you adjust the blanket under the saddle just right.
You stand as far forward as you can,
Next to the horse's left front leg.
Your eyes are watching his left back leg.
This is so that whether you are saddling a bronc,
Or even a gentle horse, who a fly might bite at the wrong time,
If he tries to jump forward with his left hind hoof,
To cow kick you in the head,
You can see that kick coming.
Then, still standing, watching for the left hind hoof,
You reach under the horse's belly
With your left hand to bring the cinch ring close.
If the horse is a bronc or mean-natured,
You may want to reach under

With a little curved stick to catch the cinch ring,
And then, push the leather latigo strap
Up past the tongue of the ring.
Then you snug up the cinch
Through the ring just a little bit at a time.
These are the movements and the habits
That will keep you safe or save your life someday,
Whether you are throwing your saddle on a bronc or a gentle horse.
Then you lead your horse forward a few steps at a time.
Then snug up the cinch a little bit again,
Then lead your horse up a little bit again,
So you don't ever get him cinch-bound and wanting to buck
'Cause you've made his poor belly sore.
Then you step onto the stirrup on either the left or right side,
With either your left or your right foot,
'Cause your left knee's so achy,
That you can't get on the left side,
Called the "near" side, all of the time.
OK, then you swing your leg over the horse's back,
And then try to ease your horse off, kinda slow,
So that he doesn't want to buck you off,
Right off, the very first thing in the morning,
Which is usually exactly what he wants to do.
Especially if he's young, or if he's feeling good,
Or if it's been a cold night,
Or if another horse has said something bad to him,
Or maybe kicked him, or maybe bit him on the ass.
Then, when you urge him forward a little,
And when he goes to loosen up a little, he begins to jog.
This is the perfect gait you want to get him to go,
As soon as possible, because if he starts to walk too much,
It gives him way too much time to think about bucking you off,
And where and when to pick a perfect place to do it.
It might only be crossing a little ditch,
That under any other set of circumstances,
He would pass right over, later in the day,
Especially if he was headed towards home.

That pace, called the jog or slow trot,
Is way different from a high trot, which is considerably faster.
The jog allows you to cover a lot of big country,
Without tiring either the horse or you too much.
It is that pace that best allows you to absorb the pounding
Of your horse's hooves on the ground.
One way to do that is to do a kind of a dance
That shifts your weight from one stirrup to the other,
In the rhythm of the horse's hooves striking the ground.
Another way to absorb the hammering of those hooves,
Is to let your shoulders and your arms and your elbows do it.
A lot of old-time cowboys ride this way.
They look a lot like birds, flapping along above the saddle,
But that way doesn't hurt a cowboy's back so much.
Some cowboys absorb the hoof beats
By moving their pelvic bones back and forth.
I like to think if you use all of these different ways just a little,
Even including leaning forward to post,
By standing up in the saddle once in a while,
Especially over rough ground,
I like to think you can get your old body,
And your horse's body, through a long day's work.
'Cause once in a while, you do put in a ten- to fifteen-hour day,
Especially if you do have to put in two days' work in one,
For one reason or another.
(Like, maybe the buyer wants the calves in the trucks a day earlier)
Anyway, that rhythm of saying each syllable of the phrase
Turquoise stones in the creek bed,
The sound of the horse's hooves in the sand
Is one that lets you cover the most country, the easiest way.
That's why I've scattered it through this book,
So you will be able to ride with me,
To give you the feel of being in the saddle,
To feel the pounding of the horse's hooves.
When you hear: *Turquoise stones in the creek bed,*
The sound of the horse's hooves in the sand,
That's the only pace that will let us get through this book together.

'Cause when that pace has been a good part of a man's life,
And a good part of his thoughts,
A great majority of his thoughts
Come from the rhythm of his horse's hooves, beating on the ground.
Then you can understand, in the pounding of a heartbeat,
Where we are going, to ride with the cowboys,
Through the deep arroyo that flows to the end of this book.

• • • • •

TURQUOISE STONES IN THE CREEK BED ...
                THE SOUND OF THE HORSE'S HOOVES IN THE SAND.

Cutting the Hide

Old Strands

Roberto was beginning to make a reata.
He sat in the middle of a fleshed,
Dried cowhide, staked to the ground.
He leaned towards the outer edge.
He began to cut the hide into a long circling strand.
It spiraled like a maze,
Towards the center of the hide.
The reata had less wind resistance.
It could be thrown further than any nylon rope.
But if a large animal was caught,
And the reata not dallied lightly, lightly,
And left to run around the saddle horn, the reata would break.
I realized that the coiling spirit of my breath was a reata,
Woven from those same strands of blood and flesh,
Old strands of the dried hides of our journey.
Dallied lightly, it might not break.

Rounding Up the Country

A Reata with Which to Gather the Lands

Where there's a bunch of cattle running
In the deserts and the mountain country,
And we want to round them up to see just who they are,
We'll need to ride out in these rangelands,
Gather them, drive them on the trails wherever they're headed,
Rope those wild mavericks who want to skitter away,
And keep them all headed towards the end of the trail.
Riding, each cowboy's got a string of horses.
We've got nothing here to ride, but strings of light words
To catch the wild spirit of this open country.
Each roundup, some chapter, tracing the light years
Across these pages that have no end,
Carrying men and wild cattle through the blue mountain ranges.
Each poem is a saddle, thrown onto the back
Of this spinning old buckskin mare called Earth
Whirling us down whatever trail we're headed.
Come on, let's go riding ...
Horses, cowboys, mules, all of the long ears listening here,
We'll catch that wild spirit of America.
We'll rope and tie it with our whirling loops,
Herd it through the pale deserts and blue mountain ranges.
We'll let it drift here in the sunlight.
We'll drive that whirling spirit home,
To leave it singing here, for you.

Vocation

Avocation

"Hey Buster Welch," says one of the young cowboys
  Who is learning to ride a cutting horse,
"Why do we have to get up at four o'clock in the mornin'?
  We never start work till six."
  Says Buster, "That's when I do my best thinkin',
  Between four and six in the mornin'."
"Well, why do we have to get up with you?"
  Says the young cowboy. Says Buster,
"I'm tryin' to teach you how to think."

—Voice of BUSTER WELCH

· · · · ·

Wood cookstove ashes scattered in the creek
Where seven arroyos bring Earth together,
At this joining place I live.
Propped on a rock, a wind at my ear,
By this deepest desert pool I lie,
Waiting for you to come near.

The Rock

Immense, ridged grey faces
Hovering above the canyon walls,
Pushed upwards out of the boiling lava.
Deep deep down,
The cauldron of the red hot Earth
Cooling before my eyes.
Twisted cedars still hanging
On the cracks of the cliff faces,
From fifty thousand years ago.
A canyon wren calling ...

The Seasons

The song of the Springtime in Guadalupe
Is the trilling song of the canyon wren.
For us who have listened, waiting,
Through drought and dryness, ice and snow
For that trilling, winged song to come,
Echoing again and again and again ...
One Springtime more, in Guadalupe.

From a High Mountain Range

To Own the Land

Roberto and Drum are riding together.
They are on the highest mountain
In the Guadalupe Range.
They are looking way off into the distances
On the furthest horizon towards the mountain range
Called La Sierra de San José.
Roberto gestures in the direction
Of those faraway mountains.
"Para allá está mi tierra.
Over there is my land," he says.
Roberto does not own the mountain range.
He is of the mountain range.
In that way he belongs to the mountains
And the mountains belong to him.
In the same way, *vaqueros* and cowboys
Belong to the lands in which they ride and work,
The big valleys and mountain ranges.
And those big valleys and mountain ranges
Belong to cowboys.
And if those cowboys act a little wild
Only once or twice
In the stretched heartstrings of a great while,
It is because they feel too much.
The shrinking loss of their lands,
The loss of their friends, the great loss
Of their deserts and blue mountain ranges.

Calling

The Light

Come on, let's go catch the morning light.
We'll climb the cliff rocks by the ridgeline trail to see
That morning light running along the ridgeline,
To see who taught the white-winged doves to sing
That sweet sound of forever,
Forever echoing along the cliff rocks in the Cajón Bonito,
Along the cliff rocks by the ridgeline trail.
Come on, are you ready?
Hurry up, let's go ...

Calling Forever

Watching the Dawnlight Come

Slow, the grey light comes running,
Along the blue lips of the Sierra Madres,
Pale stillness of cliff rocks,
Dark canyons, *bellota* oak trees.
When it's hot, we sweat.
When it's cold, we shiver.
One old bronc rider, stiff and sore,
Leads his horse, Red, over to a rock,
Steps onto the rock with his left foot,
Throws his right leg over the saddle cantle,
Goes riding away, into the dawnlight.

A Trail

Through the Dawnlight

"You can't hardly tell where this trail goes," he says.
"Just where it used to be, these rocks has rolled
   Down off the mountain cliffs in it.
   Manzanitas growed in from the sides."
   Whack, the oak brush hits him in the leg.
"Red, damn your old hide, Red, you come wrong again!
   That's right, now stop and get a bite to eat.
   Red, damn your old hide!"
   Gnats' wings, a butterfly's wings, an old cowboy passing
   On a trail through the sunlight.

—Voice of WALTER RAMSEY

• • • • •

TURQUOISE STONES IN THE CREEK BED ...
        THE SOUND OF THE HORSE'S HOOVES IN THE SAND.

COWBOYS

If you see a feller, standin' around with a big, broad-brimmed hat,
Slouched down outside of a cantina in the Borderlands,
Or maybe by the edge of a building in a little Mexican town,
If he's lookin' across the lands, towards the ends of those blue distances,
And if he looks like he's half the man he could be
Without a horse between his legs,
That feller might be a cowboy.
But you never can tell, just by lookin'.

· · · · ·

Ain't No Cure

Cowboyin' is somethin' fellers got to love
As much as whiskey or women.
If he wants money or what money can buy,
He ain't got no business bein' a cowboy.

—Voice of BILL BRYAN

Telling Time

Walter Sits on a Rock

He holds the long split leather reins
Leading to his horse's bridle
In his weathered left hand.
He is waiting for the red and blue colored shirts of the *vaqueros*.
They'll come riding down the Chulo Tank Draw.
It is during Spring roundup time.
He watches the sunlight paint, as with a brush,
The rose-colored wisps of clouds overhead,
Then the broken canyons of mesa country,
Still to the East, in the long drawn mountain shadows.
A mosquito hums and drops to the creased edge
Of Walter's thumb, while he sits in that stillness,
To watch the dawnlight come through the lowest saddle
In the mountains to the East.
It strikes the flaking, green grey lichen beside him.
It lights the red cliff rock where a withered cedar tries
To twist from the arroyo up into the light.
So many times he has watched the dawnlight come.
Says Walter, "A cowboy's mind needs to be part bronc,
Part blue mountain, part that arroyo
Where he rides his colt barefoot them first few saddles,
Winding through them soft cliff sands,
Part momma cow, part young heifer, part yearling steer,
Head held high, ready to run, tail up in the air."

Buried Treasure

A Mystery

The roundup crew of the San Bernardino Ranch
Had been asked to do two days of work in one day.
The cattle buyer needed to have the steers
In the shipping corrals of Agua Prieta,
But it was one day earlier than had been planned.
The *vaqueros* were spread out through the shimmering distances,
As far as each rider could see another,
Bobbing into view, sometimes along the horizon,
Sometimes not.
Across that great sweep of the San Bernardino Valley,
They were gathering the country
As far to the East as the arroyo of Guadalupe.
They were in the wing on a long circle.
Porfirio, Drum, and Catarino were among the *vaqueros*,
But they were on the innermost edge of the wing.
They were waiting for the other far riders
To join them in the circle.
Porfirio dismounted and began walking.
He looked very intently at the ground.
He walked around them for probably seven minutes.
They had no idea what he was doing,
Nor why he seemed so intensely interested in that earth.
Finally, he raised his head and looked up.
He scowled at them and said,
"¿No crees que el maldito indio Gerónimo? ...
Don't you think that damn Indian Geronimo
Could have left me just one gold piece here in the dirt?"
The *vaqueros* break out in smiles
They have been in the distances
And that stillness for too long.
They need to hear the sounds of laughter.

—*Voice of* PORFIRIO SOMOSA

The Cowboy's Dream

Stronger horses
Cheaper whiskey
Wilder women

Cheaper women
Wilder horses
Stronger whiskey

Wilder whiskey
Cheaper horses
Stronger women

"Well," she said, "whatever way you look at it,
It all just adds up to trouble for a woman."

—Voice of a cowboy's wife

No Way to Get Away

Cowboyin' Is Somethin' a Feller's Got to Love

There's no cure.
Just look at the fellers a-livin' around here.
They've tried prospectin', weldin', minin', rodeoin'.
They've tried smugglin', farmin', school marmin',
A-drivin' trucks, and a-workin' on cats.
There's one feller a-livin' around here,
Drives a bulldozer and a Caterpillar tractor.
Why he could turn on a biscuit and never break the crust,
And he's not a bad hand with a horse nor a mule neither.
Him and all of 'em go back to a ranch
Somewheres, runnin' a few cows,
Workin' for less than they could make
Most any place else they tried,
A-losin' their shirts when the rains don't come,
Or the price of beef drops.
They can't help it,
They've got it in their hearts.
Nope, there's no cure for cowboys.

—Voice of BILL BRYAN

Roping Your Horse Out of the Remuda

To Catch What You Want to Ride for the Day

As the horses are there, waiting, pawing their hooves in the dust,
In the early dawn, under the last stars or moon.
If you are working for a big outfit, especially in Mexico,
You will probably have to rope the horse that you will ride for the day
Out of the *remuda,* those milling cowboy mounts.
If your horse is standing still, aim to throw your loop
A little behind his head, because when he sees your loop
Coming towards him through the air,
He will try to duck the loop by stepping backwards.
Now, if your horse is moving, with the other horses in the *remuda,*
Aim to throw your loop a little ahead of the direction in which he is moving,
Because then, he will run faster to try to avoid your throw.

A Primer for Cowboys

What a Cow Knows

Some fellers can ride through a rough country
And come out with most everythin'
That's a-runnin' there. Some fellers can't.
Now a cow, first thing she'll do
When she hears you a-comin' is swing her head
Towards the sound of your horse's hooves.
The next thing she'll do is swing her head
In the direction of her calf.
She may hide that calf from you.
Sometimes it's pretty hard to find a calf
With only a few scuff marks in the sands
To help you to know if the calf is dead
And maybe has been eaten on some.
Look at that thin skin that'll cover
The calf's little hooves, when the calf is first born.
If the skin is broken, it means that the calf walked
Before some critter started eatin' on it.
If the skin isn't broken,
It means that the calf wasn't killed by no predator,
But was born dead.
If the calf isn't dead,
And you finally get the cow together with her calf,
Then keep watchin' 'cause after a while, even in brushy country,
Where you can't see very far ahead of you,
You can find the rest of her partners,
Because the next thing that cow will do
Is swing her head in the direction of her partners.
And if you don't push her too hard,
She'll lead you to where all of her partners are a-runnin'.
She's been in those mountains all Summer long.
When there's been no rain,
She knows, and her partners know,
Where the sideoats grama grasses will
Stay green in the shade of an oak,
Or near a cool cliff on the North side

Of an East-West runnin' canyon.
In Wintertime, when the ice comes
And the waters are froze, she knows the warm springs,
Where she reckons she can still drink.
In Springtime, she knows
Where the grasses will green up first,
In a corner of a *rincón,*
On the South side of a mountain,
Where two low ridges come together.
Dry times, she knows the springs
That'll stay clear the longest,
And when they muddy, she'll go away
And wait to drink till the water clears.
If you let her, she'll show you.
An old cow, she knows where she's come from
And she knows where she'll go.

         —Voice of JUAN BIDEGAIN

What a Dog Knows

Alvin Taylor and Cow Dogs

"It used to be, cowboys would talk about horses
  Doin' some pretty unusual things," Vernie Taylor says,
"But since cow dogs have come to this country,
  Now it's dogs.
The other day, Alvin Taylor and some fellers
Were tryin' to decide whose dog was best.
Those boys thought they had some pretty good dogs,
Till Alvin told about his cow dog, Jody.
Old Alvin and Jody was a-prowlin' through a rough pasture one day.
They saw two steers, looked like they was from off of another outfit.
Alvin couldn't make out the brand, so he roped one of them steers,
Tied it, and was a-wettin' that brand down to where he could read it.
The other steer took off runnin'.
Alvin told his dog Jody to go catch that steer.
Well, Alvin got the hair patted down and was able to read that brand.
He got back onto his horse and headed for where he'd last seen
Old Jody, a-runnin' that other steer over the ridge line.
When he got to the top of the hill, sure enough, old Jody
Had him laid down on the ground, and that dog was a-standin' there,
With his back leg hiked up in the air, a-peein' on that brand.
Neither Alvin nor Jody was ever much good at readin' a dry brand."

—*Voice of* VERNIE TAYLOR

• • • • •

To get a steer down, a dog will grab a steer's tender nose.

What an Inspector Knows

A Cattle Inspector Is Just Like a Woman

Well, we finally captured an old cow who'd been runnin'
Mostly on a neighbor's ranch for the past two years.
Her big heifer calf turned up missin' last year, but that's another story.
Anyway, we decided it might be best for all concerned if we sold that cow
At the Willcox Livestock Auction. But she was a roamin', gallivantin',
Fence breachin' son of a gun and we didn't know
How long we could keep her in a pasture near the home corrals.
Tried for two weeks to get ahold of the cattle inspectors,
To inspect her to go to the auction. Fernando Escalante was on vacation.
A telephone recording answered his telephone.
Sammy Eddington was overworked.
So, thinkin' she'd get away, we went ahead, and after a pretty good battle,
Loaded that cow into a two-horse trailer, headed into town.
We hoped somethin' would work things out for the best.
It did.
Stopped at the first available telephone,
Forty miles and twenty-seven creek-crossings from home.
Called Sonny Shores, the Willcox Livestock auctioneer.
Asked him if he had any ideas about getting that cow
Inspected for the next eighty miles to Willcox.
"Call John Logan, the Willcox Cattle Inspector," he says, "384-3854."
"Do you think he'll let me
Take that cow to Willcox and inspect her there?" Drum asks.
"Well," says Sonny, "you never can tell.
These cattle inspectors are kind of like a woman.
One day they will, and one day they won't."
So Drum called John Logan and explained the problem.
"Well, the Douglas inspector's getting off vacation today or tomorrow.
You really ought to talk with him before you move that cow anymore.
That, or take her the forty miles back to the ranch,
But, well, I guess maybe I could do it for you just this one time."
Goddamn, what a relief. Sometimes she will, sometimes she won't.
Today, he ... she ... did.
Yep, a cattle inspector's just like a woman.

—Voice of JOHN LOGAN

Institute of Further Studies

The Atlantic and the Pacific

Buster Welch was a-havin' some trouble
Teachin' a young woman how to ride a cuttin' horse,
Without losin' the cow she was tryin' to cut from the herd.
Her trouble was that she didn't give neither her horse
Nor the cow enough time to make a good cut.
Finally, Buster told her.
He says, "Listen honey, don't hurry your horse.
Don't hurry that cow."
Says Buster, "She can't get away.
There's an ocean on either side of her."

—Voice of BUSTER WELCH

Lovers Driving Cattle

The Cowboy and the Beautiful Dude Called Eve

Ninety percent of the world doesn't understand cowboys.
Hugh and Eve were lovers but still they had
A ways to go to really get to know one another,
To learn the subtleties of each other's ways.
They were driving together up the dirt road in a pickup truck.
They came upon nine head of brindle Brahma cross cows
When they were about a quarter of the way up the mountain.
Said Hugh, "I'm a-gonna drive them cows over there
Plum on up to the top of the mountain."
Because Eve couldn't figure out how Hugh was going to be able
To load the nine full-grown cows into the back of that pickup truck,
She asked him, "Why Hugh, how are you going to be able
To drive them nine cows up there?"
Said Hugh, turning towards her with a loving smile,
"I'm a-gonna ride a horse, and them cows are gonna walk."

—Voices of EVE PETERSON *and* HUGH

America

The Melting Pot

"This here is my compadre, Dewy Newsom,
  He's eighty-two years old," Leadford Mayo says.
"They call him Dude. He's had a stroke and lost a part of his memory.
  He forgets that part where he rustled so many cattle and stole so many horses.
  That old horse thief can't afford to remember without a-goin' to jail."
"This here's Leadford Mayo, he's sixty-eight," Dewy Newsom says.
"He's part Texan, part Irish, part Mexican, and part Cherokee blanket ass.
  He don't know how to drive a car.
  We run a few cows here so we don't go crazy."
"I've never drove a car from here to that lamp post," old Leadford says.
"Cars is what's ruined this whole damn country of America."
"Well, there's one time I wish I'd been a-drivin' one of 'em," Dude says.
"I was herdin' about seventy-two head of cows across these sagebrush flats.
  I was ridin' a mare. She was the best mare in America.
  She could foxtrot ten miles an hour and you could set on her and rest.
  Anyway, this old bunch quitter made me mad.
  I went a-lopin' to head her off, with my reins slack.
  That good mare broke in two and throwed me so high,
  I seen the saddle cantle was a way down below my feet.
  I come down on that saddle cantle and broke my hip.
  That mare went off and left me just like some of these women will today.
  She had a colt or somethin' she wanted to get back to.
  I was there till they found me."
"Damn good thing I didn't find you," says old Leadford,
"I'da shot you."
"It'd been a damn good thing if you had," Dude says.
"It sure woulda saved a lotta sufferin'."
"We'll see you," they say, two angular bent shapes,
  Their faces, maps of the rangelands, the winding trails they've crossed.
  There they go, laughin' down an old, old road.

—*Voices of* LEADFORD MAYO *and* DEWY NEWSOM

• • • • •

TURQUOISE STONES IN THE CREEK BED ...
        THE SOUND OF THE HORSE'S HOOVES IN THE SAND.

MEXICAN ROUNDUPS

How to Live

Dichos
Sayings of the vaqueros

Dime con quien andas,
Y voy a decirte quien eres.
Tell me with whom you go,
And I'll tell you who you are.

Hace más él que quiere,
Que él que puede.
The man who wants to,
Can do more than the one who can.

No hay que ir a buscar lo que no he perdido.
I don't have to go to find that which I have not lost.

To Understand

Dichos are sayings that allow ways of being,
Stories and laughter to reflect the knowledge of a people,
Of *Tata Lencho*, the broomweed, of the plants and ridges around them,
Of arroyos and desert valleys. They come from a heart
To make the heart of a man or a woman.
They tell him how to know his wife.
They tell her how to raise her children.
They tell her how to know him, when he seems not there to talk to her.
Like starlight, men and women come together,
Fleshed rays of light, atomic particles from a rising sun.

¿Para qué son pasiones si el amor se acaba?
What are passions for, if love goes away?

Vale más correr que saber.
It is better to run than to know.

Lo que pasó ya le llevó.
What has come to pass already carries one.

Él que busca, halle, y él que gana, lleva de perder.
He who searches, finds, and he who wins, goes towards losing.

La confianza mata el hombre.
Confidence kills a man.

El cementerio es un remedio para los años, la tristeza,
Los malos pensamientos, el cansancio, las reumas y el progreso.
The grave is a cure for the years, the sadness, the bad thoughts,
The weariness, the rheumatism, and progress.

Lo que no pasa en un año pasa en un segundo.
What doesn't come to pass in a year will happen in a second.

No capar los becerros, si la luna no está correcta,
Porque van a sangrar más.
Don't castrate your calves, if the moon's not right,
Because they will bleed more.

—Voice of PORFIRIO SOMOSA

November *Corrida*, 1971, at the Beginning of the Mexican Roundups

Porfirio sings,
"El veintiocho de noviembre presente lo tengo yo,
Que en el rancho Los Chirriones la corrida comenzó."
Swish, swish, swish,
The sound of the wind in the grama grasses ...
By the corrals of El Dormido in Sonora, Mexico,
We sit watching the clouds go past,
The planet spinning somewhere in space,
While Porfirio's horse paws the ground two times with his hoof.
The billow-like wings of a raven
Whish past us, flowing to the West.
And the mornings of the days of the roundup come,
Like beautiful old ladies of the night in Agua Prieta,
Who slowly paint eye shadows onto their faces,
And step out from the darkened shadows of their rooms,
To stand by their doorways waiting ....

Loss

Roberto Espinosa

Roberto, straight black Indian hair greying.
Gangly arms hanging at his sides,
Slightly hunched neck, nose like a beak.
Levi's fading, flower print shirt fading.
A *mayordomo*'s son *caporal*, foreman
Of the Los Chirriones Ranch roundup.
In the morning when they saw Roberto
Coming towards them,
The horses would neigh to him.
His dark skin, his dark brown eyes,
The gentleness of a woman soft in his voice,
As he tells each *vaquero* what canyons
And mesas to ride on this roundup
That will be that *vaquero*'s circle for the day.

Then Turn 'Em Out

"Haze 'em, *hijo de la chingada!*"
Two seven-year-old longhorns
Go jumping over the barbwire fence.
There go three just-weaned steer calves.
Maybe they'll forget to run back
To where they sucked their mommas last.
There go four *vaqueros*, spurring after them,
But to jump the barbwire would be suicide.
"*Déjalas jodidos,*" Roberto calls,
"Let 'em go or we'll lose all the rest."
So we light out, our horses lathered, lining out the steers,
Headed towards the old trail West towards Agua Prieta,
To sell those steers at the border shipping corrals.

—Voice of ROBERTO ESPINOSA

A First Roundup

Martín

Holding with the stance of his body,
The shuffling *remuda* of *vaquero* mounts,
Their dark shapes milling, nickering
On the South side of the Corral de Palos,
The tatters of his flowered shirt,
Tatters of his white straw hat catching the pale light.

The Horse Wrangler

Martín is fifteen years old.
He is our horse wrangler on his first roundup.
We are gathering cattle from Pitaicache peak.
We are driving them to the North,
To wait at the San Bernardino Ranch.
There, we cut the heifers away from the steers,
To let those just-weaned steers settle down a week or so,
Before making the long drive to the border shipping corrals.
"*Qué bonito está el pueblo*," Martín calls,
When we top the ridgeline and can see the town,
After a month of cactus, rough canyons,
Our horses are all run down.
Lights, white smoke from the copper smelter,
Streaming out in the Spring nighttime, West of the town.
Corridos to sing by the starlight, the darkness.

—Voice of MARTÍN

The Song of the Night

Martín and the Roundup

El veintiocho de febrero presente lo tengo yo,
Que en el Rancho los Chirriones la corrida comenzó.
hooooooo ha whistling whirrrrrrrr
"Hay que gritar, chiflar, cantar, Martín, que te oigan."
Two hundred eighty-six head of Mexico steers
In the darkness somewhere ahead of us.
"You've got to sing, yell, and whistle, Martín,
So the cattle will hear you," old Everisto calls.
Hooves clacking, cowboys singing,
Birds in the nighttime, twittering up from their roosts,
Flying by the steers' hooves.
The sounds of the *vaqueros* passing,
Singing for the cattle,
Singing for their compañeros,
Singing for the hours we'd ridden in that twisting starlight,
The night, the old Earth's still circling soul.
The country we'd seen by daylight was gone,
Only the pale faces of steers,
If a cloud didn't cross the stars,
When a steer swung his head, to look back.
Each rider wandering alone,
Vaqueros singing across the starlight, in the darkness.

—*Voice of* EVERISTO WASICA

Another Loss

To Have and to Have Not

Ah, Martín, horse wrangler for that roundup seven years ago,
Why did you come to Guadalupe?
To ask me for work and carry off my quirt and spurs?
To leave a folded gunnysack on the board where they'd been.
"Old Martín, I guess he's kinda like
One of them tradin' pack rats," Bud says.
"Hay que gritar, chiflar, cantar, Martín, que te oigan,"
Drum hears old Everisto calling across those years,
"You've got to yell and whistle and sing for the cattle,"
For the *vaqueros*, for the years of roundups
You've ridden, when those clouds crossed the starlight,
So we will hear you calling across that darkness, Martín.

—Voices of BUD ROBBINS *and* EVERISTO WASICA

THE HORSES

Staking Out the Horses

Cuando los federales me agarraron,
When the federales caught me,
They tied my hands together.
They tied me to a tree,
Me dieron toques,
They gave me shocks with a cattle prod.
I didn't tell them anything,
But I don't want to tie a horse to a stake at night.

—*Voice of* ROBERTO ESPINOSA

• • • • •

TURQUOISE STONES IN THE CREEK BED ...
        THE SOUND OF THE HORSE'S HOOVES IN THE SAND.

Quick Hooves Running

15,000 B.C.

Shapes of horses painted on the rocks.
The Neolithic hunters following their tracks.
Over the flowing waters, dried lips of arroyo sands.
From those cave paintings of Lascaux and Font-de-Gaume
Born, lived, fought, died,
Becoming cowboys headed North, up the Rio Grande.

Crossing

From the brown, dreaming steppe lands of Persia,
Empires of gold and horses, the Mongols, and Genghis Khan,
Across mountains and oceans, long grasses
Bending in the stretch of the stretching, great plains.
Pintos, sorrels, duns, bays, buckskins,
Their hooves a-running, running past desert trails,
Turquoise rocks in arroyo sands, racing by wild rivers,
Through these snowy mountain rangelands.
Running wild calls, nostrils snorting, whistling,
Across the mountains, the desert sands.
An Indian's whoop,
A cowboy's rope, to settle the West of America.
Our souls riding along beside them,
Carrying men and the weight of men,
Men and women, that pack of wild dreams ...
Horses Horses Horses

Horses and Cowboys

To Be Horseback

Sitting on top of a dun horse,
Feeling his legs running underneath you,
Feeling all that he is at the touch of a rein,
Ready to whirl or set up on a dime,
Ready to carry us across blue mountain ranges,
Ready to cross *barrancas* and arroyos,
Ready to fly when we take down our rope
To catch any wild heifer
Who breaks to run when we want her,
Ready to stop, to stay, still listening,
For whatever it is we're waiting to hear,
Feeling the beat of that pounding breath,
Hooves and heart whirling under you,
That's what it's like to be horseback.
That's what it's like to be a cowboy.

Leavings

Old Walter Ramsey

"Now what you left out," says Walter Ramsey,
"Is when you're a-ridin' a horse who'll handle like that,
 And when you go to throw your saddle onto his back
 And when you rake that frost off first,
 One of these cold Winter mornin's,
 You'll go off a-pitchin' and liable to find yourself
 A-layin' there on that cold, hard ground
 After a pretty wild bronc ride,
 And the other cowboys a-hollerin',
 'Whoo, ha,' into the dawnlight,
 They'll be just a-settin' there on their horses.
 They'll be a-lookin' down at you a-laughin'.
 And that's what it's like to get bucked off.
 And that's what it's like to be a cowboy too."

Two Poems for My Old Friend Charlie Gone Gone Gone

When Drum was an unknown kid about twenty-three years old, his friend Charles Olson said, "Could I put two of your poems into my Maximus Poems?*" One of these was Drum's poem called "Psyche" and the other was "The Range." "I did for you what no one has ever done before," said Olson to Drum. Charles Olson had a wonderful sense of humor. He laughed and he said, "One of us is going to make it and take the other one along with him," meaning that if one was famous he would make the other famous too. So Drum was returning Charles's favor when he dedicated these two horseback poems to his old friend.*

Horse Wrangling

Old Pinto horse, for twenty-three years,
You've pounded the rocks of this outfit.
A horse past fourteen can't hardly stand a day's hard work.
We've got twenty-two horses, about eight too many old ones,
Your time has come to go,
Old Pinto, looking pretty thin, standing under a mesquite.
Too thin to make it through this dry, cold Winter.
Maybe two inches of rain all Summer,
No green grass on the canyon sides or the hills.
Pinto lets the other horses take off.
I come riding towards Pinto, down a canyon side,
Thinking maybe this dry Summer's got him,
Thinking he can't make it home.
The other horses have gone.
They are maybe a quarter mile away, down the trail.
Slow, Pinto comes out from under his mesquite,
Picking up speed,
"Whoooooo ha hidda!" I call,
When I top out on the ridgeline, I can see Pinto running,
Where he belongs,
The oldest, toughest, savviest horse still on this outfit,
Loping to get wherever he's going,
Leading the horse herd along the cliffs
By the ridgeline trail,
Loping to be there at the head of 'em all.

A Good-bye for My Friend

Partners

Old horses, women, and men,
The bones of old gone loves, now, turned out to pasture.
They were my friends, they were our partners,
They were all the long trails we rode along together,
Feet in the stirrups to gather our old beginnings,
To come to some new way.
They were that flesh we are between our legs.
They were every cowboy's hope,
To do no work that couldn't be done a-horseback,
Feet in the stirrups, two legs dangling ...
Dangling from the high withers on a horse's back,
Across the mesas and arroyos, across the mountains, the plains.
In cold times they were always the two of us together,
Tail to tail, rumps turned against the wind,
Hair frosted, soft-nosed breath to breathe into your chest,
Winds of Winter and ice, till beginning in Springtime,
We were head to tail through the dryness, the droughts,
Till in those blasts of the Summertime heat,
We were that nicker, a swish of our partner's tail,
To brush the black flies from our wet eyes away.
Now, we cross this dust to stand beside you here,
Each of us alone in this last field in the light.
We come carrying a small switch.
It is made of a leaf-stripped seep willow limb.
In this searing Summer's sun we come,
To brush the black flies,
From the corners of your wet eyes away.
Good-bye old partner.
Good-bye, those bones of old gone loves,
Still here, waiting to cross in this stillness,
Feet in the stirrups, two legs dangling ...

A Last Saddle

Letting Go in the Dawnlight

Let go, Tom, let your saddle and bridle go.
Let go, Tom, of all the men and women you were.
Let go, Tom, of who we all were together,
Carousing, drinking, telling lies, and funny stories.
Turn your best horses out to pasture, Tom.
See those blue mountain ranges lying in the dawnlight.
They're where we all began and where we all will go.
Let go of the Animas Mountains, Tom.
Let go of Indian Canyon, let go of the old Adobe Camp.
Let go of the Godfrey, let go of the Lynch.
All of your friends are waiting there,
By those blue mountain ranges, lying in the dawnlight.
They're waiting to take you in.
Let go Tom, let go Tom, let go Tom
Let go.

• • • • •

Tom was a Gray Ranch cowboy from 1960 to 2002.

Gentling Colts

Without Being Told

"There are many ways to gentle a colt," says Roberto.
"Cada maestro tiene su libro.
Each teacher has his own book.
That is why in *los ranchitos chicos*, in the little ranches,
Better horses were made than on the large ranches.
On the large ranches, the *mayordomo*, the head roundup boss,
Told a *vaquero* what bit or hackamore to use and how to handle a horse.
In *los ranchitos chicos*, in the little ranches,
A *vaquero* gentled the horse he rode,
Y nadie le dijo nada. And no one told him anything.
That is how to gentle a horse, *un hombre y una mujer*, a man and a woman,
Only the lover and the loved one know."

—Voice of ROBERTO ESPINOSA

A Trail to Nowhere

Horse's Hooves

I.

Horses have been my life, horses and stock dogs.
You know a man can get to feelin' kind of *triste*.
Dry times, sometimes, his spirit will get pretty low.
But if he'll go jingle up a smooth travelin' horse,
Throw his saddle onto that horse's back,
And strike out jinglin' along ...
Maybe just followin' a trail along to nowhere,
Those hooves clickin' pretty soon
Will make his spirit start a-prancin'.
Then that ache in a man's heart will be behind him,
Blowin' away with the dust in the road.
But there's nothin', nothin' colder
Than the ashes of an old fire.

II.

Another way I've found,
To help you to remember, or to help you to forget,
Is to sit waitin' on the edge of an arroyo in Summertime,
Till a sound touches your ear that seems so far away, so faint, so light
That it might only be the wind, blowin' in the leaves.
Or is it the hollow sound
Of a horse's shod hooves, rollin' the canyon rocks,
Comin' closer and closer down the canyon?
Then suddenly, the waters of the flash flood
Are swirlin' around your feet,
And you have to step quick to decide
Which side of the swellin' waters you wish to be on,
Before the wall of the waters comes roarin' past.
If you want somethin' to come to you,
Sit and watch the waters comin' towards you.
If you want somethin' to go from you,
Sit and watch the waters flowin' away.
If you can let them,
Your thoughts will go with those waters
That have come towards you, then gone by you,
To disappear down an arroyo bend, away.
In the Wintertime, it is easier,
Because the clear waters are more steady,
And you don't have to wait so long for them
To come carry away the pain
Of your sadness.

• • • • •

*Can't remember his name, but he was raised
in the Davis Mountains of West Texas*

The Journey

Who We Are

Old trees that have stood here,
Through these storms, for hundreds of years,
One windy day, we all fall down.
"*Híjole*," says Roberto, "some days,
We don't even need the wind."

—*Voice of* ROBERTO ESPINOSA

Querencia

For a Mule Going Home

Three passing Mexicans came to Guadalupe to ask for work.
There was work to string a drift fence across a saddle,
Way off high by Cloverdale peaks. They took the gentle mule, Mike.
They packed him with all of their gear.
They packed him with food enough for a week.
With wire and fence stretcher tools, it was a heavy load.
High up in those mountains they made a camp near the saddle.
They tied the gentle mule, Mike, to an oak limb.
But there was a small hole in the frayed bark of the oak limb,
Where the honeybees' wings
Were passing in that sunlight, in and out of the hole in the oak.
Mike stamped the ground with his hooves and kicked.
They heard him in the night.
"But that is what a mule does," they said.
"A mule stamps the ground and kicks to go back home to his *querencia*,
To that place where he wants to be, in the heart of his own home country."
At morning, standing, still tied to the oak limb,
The mule had been stung to death.
The honeybees' wings
Were still passing through that sunlight in and out
Of the frayed hole in the oak bark.
"But that is what a mule does," the men said.
"Now he has gotten away from us again.
Now the light glazes in his dark eyes to get away.
Already he laughs at us, looking back over his left shoulder.
His light hooves are clattering down the arroyo rocks towards home."

—Voice of a mule called Mike

• • • • •

TURQUOISE STONES IN THE CREEK BED ...
        THE SOUND OF THE HORSE'S HOOVES IN THE SAND.

THE OUTLAWS

The Closed Rein

A *vaquero* was killed in El Alamo this side of Altar.
His horse threw him and his foot caught in *la falsa rienda*,
The closed rein.
The horse drug him about two miles.
Estaba en pedazos.
His body was in pieces.

—*Voice of* ROBERTO ESPINOSA

When We Found Him

Estación de Tránsito en Hermosillo

Ramón Varela's horse was buckin' with him.
Ramón saw an oak limb ahead.
He leaned over to one side to go under the oak limb.
His horse had him then,
Because Ramón couldn't get back up into the saddle.
He was thrown in front of his horse.
The horse's two front hooves
Landed on Ramón's two thighs.
The thighs broke.
When we found him,
He was crawlin' along on his back with his hands.
If you go to the Estación de Tránsito in Hermosillo,
You'll see him there.
He sells books from a wheelchair.
They had to cut off his legs.

—*Voice of* ROBERTO ESPINOSA

Eternity

In the Brush Country

South of the San Bernardino Ranch,
A *vaquero* was ridin' a buckskin colt.
He roped a calf to doctor it and the colt started buckin'.
The colt threw him *y se enredó en la piola,*
And his hand got caught in the coils of the rope.
He was dragged till his head hit a limb.
No one saw it, only the traces of the tracks.
He left the ranch at sunup and when he didn't come back,
At evening, we went to look for him.
Ramón Morales was the one who found him.
I don't know,
But I think he was the father of the *mojado*, Rafael Quijada,
He, who comes by here, drunk all of the time.

—Voice of ROBERTO ESPINOSA

Never Trust a Gentle Horse

"El mayordomo de Cocóspera se lo mató en otro modo,
The foreman of the Cocóspera Ranch
Was killed another way," says Roberto.
"His spur got caught in the tail of a dun mare.
The mare started bucking.
She bucked over a bank and fell on top of him.
The saddle horn *se enteró,*
It buried itself in his stomach and he died two hours later.
It was a mare he was riding *y muy mansita la yeguita,*
She was very gentle, and he always liked to say,
'Never trust a gentle horse.'"

—Voice of ROBERTO ESPINOSA

A Long-Tailed Horse

I never did like a long-tailed horse and I'll tell you why.
One time, over on the Diamond A,
Old Diefe Hewett was a-ridin' a bronc.
Well, it was in the Fall of the year.
There was a mess of cockleburs that year.
There was some that was hooked in that bronc's tail.
His tail was long and tangled.
Old Diefe went to get offa that bronc,
Just as he was a-swingin' his leg over the horse's rump,
That bronc swished his tail.
The tail hair caught in the spur on old Diefe's right leg.
Well, old Diefe was as good as dead,
'Cause there wasn't no way he coulda got his spur loose,
To get offa that bronc,
And there wasn't no way he coulda rode that bronc,
With his spur caught in the tail hair neither.
Lee Taylor happened to be a-standin' near.
He was a-lookin' at Diefe just when it happened.
The bronc made a jump,
Old Lee spurred his horse up.
He grabbed that bronc by the hackamore rein,
Just when the bronc was startin' in to buck and run.
And you know, they had to cut that spur out with a knife,
To get it to come free of the tail.
No sir, I never did like a long-tailed horse.

—Voice of WALTER RAMSEY

Spurs

Under the Horse's Hooves

"We were shippin' cattle in the Fall," says Warner Glenn.
"John Magoffin had come to the Malpai Ranch to help.
He was ridin' a young horse.
Daddy was ridin' an old, broke, gentle thing.
A calf slipped out of the corrals.
John didn't want to go to rope him
Off of that young green colt,
So old Daddy dropped a loop over the calf's head,
Just like he'd done hundreds of times before.
But the calf turned and the horse whirled,
And the rope went under the horse's tail.
And that gentle horse
Went to spinnin', and pitchin', and buckin'.
Old Daddy was doin' a pretty fair job a-ridin',
Till his horse bucked into the fence.
The horse caught a hind foot in the barbwire.
Daddy loosened up,
Thinkin' that horse was a-goin' to fall.
But the horse didn't fall, he kept on buckin'.
But Daddy was loose.
His spur drove into that hole in the saddle,
Just behind the saddle swells and the horn.
He was caught by that spur.
He was hung from the side of the saddle.
Then the horse's hind hoof jerked free of the fence.
That gentle horse took to runnin' off
Across the bare Malpai country.
I saw Daddy's old, bald head a-bouncin' along,
Under the horse's hooves, across those black lava rocks.
I thought old Daddy was dead,
But his foot pulled free of his boot after a while.
He fell clear of the horse's hooves.
That saved him.
He don't wear spurs very often now.

—Voice of WARNER GLENN

The Cowboy and a Rattlesnake

It Ain't No Use to Fool with Him No More

"One time I was a-drivin' a bunch of cattle into Willcox.
 I was startin' to roll me a cigarette," says Walter,
"When that bronc I was a-ridin' snorted.
 He turned right back under me and went to buckin'.
 I lost my hat, my cigarettes, my hackamore rein came in two.
 I come pretty near gettin' bucked off.
 I stepped offa that bronc,
 I gathered up my outfit, I tied my hackamore rein back together,
 Climbed back on that bronc, and I never rode fifty yards,
 Before he done the same thing again.
 He bucked back and forth over a rattlesnake twice.
 Old Boozer Page said if that hadda been a good horse,
 That rattlesnake woulda bit him,
 You know, that bronc bucked seventeen times
 Between the ranch and Willcox.
 He was a blue, blazed-faced bronc we called Old Baldy.
 When I come on into Willcox,
 That horse just went a-buckin' down the street.
 He bucked through that whole bunch of cattle.
 He scattered cows and calves ever which way.
 When we got back to the ranch, old Boozer Page told me,
 'Turn him loose. I don't know what I'll do with him,
 But it ain't no use to fool with him no more.'"

—Voice of WALTER RAMSEY

HORSE BREAKING

There's never a horse that's never been rode,
There's never a cowboy that's never been throwed.

A Cowboy in Time

When I came out of the barn, the mornin' sunlight
Was just a-comin' over Saddle Gap Mountain.
The last thing I remember was a-steppin' onto that bronc.
When I came to, it was evenin'.

—Voice of WALTER RAMSEY

· · · · ·

TURQUOISE STONES IN THE CREEK BED ...
                THE SOUND OF THE HORSE'S HOOVES IN THE SAND.

Seven Saddles

The old way that a bronc comes to be a usin' horse
Is to have a few blankets and a saddle thrown on him
And a cowboy slips into that saddle
To see if that bronc can be rode.
In cowboy lingo, the number of times
That a colt has been ridden
Is referred to as the number of saddles
That have been thrown on his back.
If a bronc had been ridden seven times,
A cowboy would say he's got seven saddles on him.

Heart

"Goddamn, that little bay colt I been keepin' for a stud
Is the buckin'est, kickin'est, rarin'est, pitchin'est bronc
I've ever started," Drum says to Bill Bryan one day in town.
"He bucks so much with just the saddle on,
You can't hardly stay in the corral with him.
There's just hooves a-flyin' at you,
Every which way you turn to break and run.
I think I'll cut off his balls.
Don't want that buckin' passed on to all my mares and colts."
"Wait a little bit," Bill Bryan says,
"If he keeps it up, cut him.
But a bronc like that sometimes
Will sure make you a darn good horse.
I'll bet he's smart too.
Don't fault him on it startin' those first few saddles.
It's somethin' extra. That bronc's got heart."

A Cold-Jawed, Steel Dust Horse

Well, Lee Howard and me was a-sittin' on our horses.
We were holdin' up a bunch of cattle.
It was under those oak trees, above the spring, up Tanque Creek.
Lee was a-tellin' some story about a horse.
He always had a bunch of mares.
He raised a few colts and was a-horse-tradin' around.
He was tellin' about the time he was ridin'
A cold-jawed, Steel Dust horse.
He couldn't do nothin' with him.
He couldn't turn him to the right nor to the left,
Nor stop him neither.
That horse was just a-flyin' along a-runnin' full tilt.
He was a-headin' for some brush and mesquite thickets.
Lee got so mad, he took his big knife.
He said to himself, "I'm just gonna cut that son of a bitch's throat."
He reached up around the horse's neck to cut the throat,
But that horse was a-runnin' so fast, it was kind of hard to cut his throat.
Just as he went to make the cut, that horse gave a lurch.
Old Lee cut his horse's bridle in two.
He turned his horse plumb wild loose.

—Voice of WALTER RAMSEY

The Compassionate Teachings of Billy Brown

How to Teach a Horse to Stop

"Billy," I ask him, "How do you teach a horse to stop ...
   And slide on his back feet,
   And leave those marks like 11's in the dust?"
"Well, all this goddamn schoolin' a lotta people do
   Doesn't do a horse a damn bit of good," he says.
"If you want to teach a horse to stop ... you just stop him ...
   When you need to get off, to take a shit, or a piss."
"Billy, do I have this hackamore set right?
   I guess I really oughta take another wrap on that *bosal*,
   And slant it a little lower under her chin."
"Aw hell," Billy says, "All these fine points
   Don't really mean anythin',
   Just so long as you get it on her head
   Instead of on her ass."
   The last lesson—
   Getting to the heart of the teachings...
"Billy, just exactly what are you doing when you say you're just
   Walking that blue horse up and down the canyon?
   Are you getting him to tuck his chin and flex his neck?"
"Well goddamn," says Billy Brown, "if you can't see it,
   There's no damn use in tellin' you."

—Voice of BILLY BROWN

Not to Miss a Lick

A Filly Colt and a Fart

That old Lee Robbins, he don't miss a lick.
Lee was puttin' three-way hobbles
Onto the legs of a filly colt he was a-breakin'.
She made a jump to get away,
When he'd only got one hobble on her.
Them hobbles was a-swingin' and a-clackin'
And a-whackin' her on her heels.
She started to make a run to jump that high pipe gate.
Old Lee, he knew he had her then.
"Whoa," Lee yelled,
Just when she hit the top rail of that high pipe gate.
She was a-fallin' back into the corral,
It looked like she was about to break her neck.
"Whoa, WHOA," Lee yelled.
She hit the ground with all four feet straight in the air,
And when she hit, she farted,
But when she got up, she nickered,
And she was a-comin' to him across the corral.
That old Lee Robbins, he don't miss a lick.

—Voice of BILL BRYAN

Courtship
Whiskey and Horses and Wild, Wild Women

They'll Drive You Crazy, They'll Drive You Insane

"Drink has ruined a lot of good men," Bill Bryan says.
"It's ruined a lot of better men than the ones who it couldn't ruin."
"Now, when you're ridin' a string of horses," Bill Bryan says,
"You'll usually find there's one thing that each of those
  Horses can do pretty well. He may not do a lot of things,
  But if you can find that one thing he can do well,
  And let him do it, both you and he will be a lot happier.
  The main thing about breakin' horses is, as you get older,
  It takes longer to do the work... Just like a woman.
  It takes you all night to do what you used to do all night.
  But really, in the long run, who knows,
  You may get as much or more done, gentlin' 'em, I mean.
  Some horses are just natural born sortin' horses,
  They can go into a herd and pick one steer out
  And come out with that steer every time and hardly
  Disturb any of the others in the herd.
  Like old Pete Middleton says, 'Some women
  Can go into a mob of men, sort 'em out, and separate 'em
  Exactly as they want 'em, and take that man
  Off without causin' a ripple.'"

Master and Apprenticeship

Rattlesnake Bit

Why, I'd rather a horse of mine get rattlesnake bit,
Than to have one of them boys a-ridin' him.
You can doctor a horse for a snake bite.
He'll maybe have a chance to get over it,
But you let one of them boys ride him,
That's the end for him.
He's had it. There's no cure.

—Voice of LEE ROBBINS

Beto's Colt

El Tumbador

Horseback hazing for Beto, holding his five-year-old bronc
By the hackamore lead rope, while Beto tries to swing
A leg over the bronc's back to get his foot down
Into that faraway stirrup on the off side.
The bronc's nose quiverin', flanks tremblin' ...
Snortin', and rarin', and runnin'
Backwards and forwards and buckin' sideways.
"Goddamn, how am I goin' to get loose from all this?
I feel a poem comin' on," thinks Drum.
Dar la vuelta ... take a few turns of that rope around the saddle horn.
That'll stop that bronc for a couple of seconds.
Beto swings his leg over, pulls the blindfold
From the colt's poppin', wide eyes, and the wreck is on again.
Beto hollerin', "Whoa ... whoa ..."
The bronc spinnin', and buckin'.
Juniper the cowdog helpin' out the only way she knows,
Barkin' and bitin' the colt on his heels.
Then she shifts over to Drum's blue hazin' horse when she figures
She's got El Tumbador's heels just a-flyin' pretty high.
"Whoa ... whoa ..."
Whoooooooo ha! There goes Beto's sombrero.
There goes Beto followin' it down.
That's three times he's lost his hat,
And only got bucked off once.
"*Trae otro caballo*," Beto laughs,
  From the yellow leaves on the ground,
"Bring another hazing horse."
"Get Humperdink for a hazin' horse," Bud says.
"He's sure gonna get somebody hurt one of these days."
  But there's nothin' else around the corral to ride,
  And El Tumbador's got to be hazed somewhere this evening,
  After buckin' around so pretty.
  Saddled up old Humperdink, and took off again.
  Made it home safe with the sun goin' down.
  Yellow ash leaves fallin'.

The sheep and the milk cows comin' in to the barn.

A woodpecker callin' off to the South

Twick, twick, twick

But the next day, we're ready for 'em.

Just at morning, when we're fresh, we'll ride these colts.

Beto rides El Tumbador twelve miles

Down to the Puerta Blanca and back.

Got his lead rope in my hand so when he trys to buck,

I can maybe jerk him up out of it and give Beto a chance.

"I'm gettin' like Bud," Beto says,

"Hay que cuidar el cuerpo más,

I've got to start takin' care of my body more."

The bronc just trys to buck three times.

Hell, he can't.

We're takin' him so fast he can't think about anything

Except his clackin' hooves just a-flyin' along down the road.

"*Ya está*, I think we got him," Beto says. "*Está aflojándose,*

He's loosenin' up after we've run and jogged him about ten miles."

Goddamn, we need more

Old, unbroken, Mexican outlaw broncs around here.

Gives us something to talk about when we come in at dinner time.

"*Ya está la comida*, now the food is ready" Maria calls.

We laugh, can't eat for a while.

Too much galloping through all these falling leaves and the sunlight.

Beto's colt, El Tumbador.

RODEOIN'

The Rewards of Rodeo Cowboys

As one of them rodeo cowboys said,
When he come a-blastin' out of the ropin' box,
At the rodeo grounds in Cheyenne, Wyoming,
Roped his calf, flung his slack, flew down the rope,
Tied that calf in twelve seconds flat,
Flung his hands up into the air...
"By God, I just knew the panties was a-gonna come,
Just a-sailin' into that arena."

—Voice of an unknown rodeo cowboy

Alone

The Rangeland Cowboy

You take one of these rodeo cowboys
Who thinks he's a bronc rider.
Send him off to make a circle alone
On one of them broncs who's a-lookin'
Around at him kind of sideways all day,
Till that boy gets tired and loosens up a little.
Then that bronc farts and gives a snort.
He goes buckin' off down one of these *lechugilla* ridges.
Why, that horse's maybe just gettin' started in eight seconds.
We'll see if that boy's a cowboy or not,
'Cause there's nobody there to come
To pick him off of that bronc after his eight seconds is up,
And there's nobody to see him,
When he's all alone, a-hangin' them spurs in on his ride.

—*Voice of* WALTER RAMSEY

• • • • •

In rodeo competition, a man must come into the arena out of the chute gate, spurring his horse, and stay on that horse until eight seconds have passed. In the rangelands, a cowboy's alone and there are no rules for a horse or a man and there are rocks, cliffs, tree limbs, and lechugilla *plants that a horse'll use to kill you. The English name for* lechugilla *is Spanish dagger. You sure wouldn't want to get bucked off in it.*

Arena Competition

A Steer-Ropin' Head Loop

Boom, you come out of the box.
Swish, swish, swish ...
Be careful,
Nobody can hear better than a steer.
They hear the swish of that loop
Above them, swingin' through the air.
Those steers thatta been roped before,
They'll get to duckin' their heads, 'cause to win,
Most boys'll throw at 'em on that third swing.
Now the faster a steer is,
And the faster you have to be to win,
The greater the angle you take
Up the arena after you've roped him.
You set your horse and the steer cracks.
If he's a runaway, you move back up the arena.
If he's slow, you just fade down.
Every header has to have three different loops:
One for way wide steers,
One for steers runnin' under your horse's neck,
And that home run shot, perfect position.
There are three distances—
Reach, normal, and extra close.
Every time you rope,
You're throwin' nine different situations.
Be careful,
When you're throwin', don't leave the circle.
You're lookin' through the loop.
Those steers know they're gonna get their necks stretched.
Most of them'll duck on that third swing.
Remember, nobody can hear better than a steer.

—Voice of CLAY LYNCH

Rodeoin'

"Listen boy," Joe tells thirteen-year-old Seth,
"When you rope that calf and tie him,
 You run to jump on your horse.
 Ride him two steps forward till that rope slacks.
 You see those guys walkin' kind of slow
 With their arms bowed out after they've tied a calf.
 That walk says, 'Hey, look at me, I'm an RCA cowboy.'
 When you see that walk, you know
 That boy ain't got nothin' goin' for him.
 Rodeoin' used to be cowboys and ranch horses,
 Now it's athletes and race horses.
 You run to your horse, jump on him.
 You're an athlete,
 Go get the money!"

Heelin' Steers

Point your loop down ...
Right at that spot you want
To hit between his legs.
Swing that loop
On the left side of your horse,
And as you turn your horse
To the left into the steer
That loop'll flatten out.
SWISH ... SWISH ... Put it in there
A two footer ... Draw your slack.
Go get the money!

Calf-Ropin' Dismount to the Left

Boom, you come out of that box.
Swish, swish,
When you're swingin' that rope,
Don't leave the circle of the loop.
Whack,
Stick it on him.
Don't move,
Drive that left knee into your horse,
Left hand to the neck,
Right hand onto the top of the horn,
Kick that right leg back,
Up and over the saddle cantle.
Still without movin' the upper part of your body,
Still with no weight on the left stirrup,
Whizz,
Your body melts to the ground,
Left foot, still in stirrup, but with no weight,
Right foot hits the ground,
You're lookin' into the saddle.
Now here's where you gain speed.
Left hand still on the mane,
Right hand still on the top of the horn.
Now throw your arms,
Your whole body into a dead run,
First step is on the left foot as it's comin' off of the saddle.
Left foot hits on the left side of the rope.
Right foot hits on the right side of the rope.
It's boom out of the box,
Swish, swing, don't leave that circle of the loop.
Whack.
Stick it on him.
Rrrrrip.
Jerk your slack.
Whizz,
Down the rope.
Go get the money.

—*Voice of* CLAY LYNCH

Rodeoing

Heroes

Great heroic people, they're the bottom of the barrel.
They're scum.
Ken Lagstrom, calf ropin' champion, he has to carry a gun.
Bert Bullard, steer ropin' champion, everybody hates him.
He stands back of the chutes when Duncan is about to rope,
He's back there cluckin', or he says,
"Hey Duncan, don't miss, you've got to support a wife."
Farley is fifth in the country in calf ropin'.
He's a kleptomaniac.
Every time I go into a store with him, when we go out,
I have to say, "OK Farley, empty your pockets."
He steals stuff worth twenty-five cents.
They're all striving for power, just like Napoleon.
Heroes, shit, they're the bottom of the barrel.

—Voice of CLAY LYNCH

A Roping

Drinking Cowboys

Well one time old Everett Campbell was
Drinkin' and ropin' for two days at Mobley's arena.
He hadn't been able to hit his hat.
Then he tilted the bottle of whiskey to his lips
One more time. He said, "Well boys,
I guess I'm ready now.
I'll match anybody here to a horse race,
A foot race, a wrastlin' match, you name it."
Well, the other cowboys who were at the ropin'
Seen old Everett just a-standin' there
With his hat on sideways,
His hair all down in his eyes.
He was a-laughin'.
He was a-wavin' fists full of dollars.
They thought, "Well, goddamn,
We'll just have to take that feller's money."
Hell, old Everett, he sacked 'em all out.
I'll bet he won over five hundred dollars that day.
All he needed was a couple of days
To get drunk and not worry about it ...

Enough to be able to do it.

—Voice of BILL BRYAN

Arena Cutting Horse Competition

Just Another Clearing

All the people watching and that fake cowboy setup there.
"Don't worry about it," old Buster Welch says,
"When you go ridin' alone, into that cuttin' arena,
Just pretend you're horseback in a little clearin',
Way off in a blue mountain range.
There's rocks and oak brush around the edge
Of that clear place.
There's an open, twelve-foot gate in the middle.
It's the only clearin' in all those blue mountains.
That's how come they put the gate there.
You've been a-hazin' along a wild,
Gallivantin', hide-out cow.
Till now, there's just she and you,
Alone, in front of that gate.
It seems like it's taken you a lifetime to find her.
You sure don't want to let her get away,
'Cause daylight's fadin',
And you've used up all the tricks you know.
If she gets away this time, she'll be gone forever.
So, sit up straight in your saddle,
Hold those split reins light,
Follow that wildness, a-dancin' in her eyes,
A leg each side of your horse's back,
A mind in the middle.
Be invisible,
Be not there.
Now drive her through that openin', twelve-foot gate.
Everywhere you go,
Ridin' alone into one of these new arenas,
Remember it's always just another clearin',
Way off in a blue mountain range.

—Voice of BUSTER WELCH

Sixteen Hundred River Road

Well, I calf-roped and steer-roped and clowned for some years.
Then, when I was workin' for Vernon Hawkins' Lazy FZ Rodeo Company,
I had a wreck.
I was one of the pickup men.
The bronc rider's horse bucked over the top of my horse.
The other boy was killed. He lived for three days, then he died.
I was pretty dingy for about eight hours.
I never have been able to remember what happened.
Went to see the boy's parents 'cause I felt pretty bad.
They were sure good. Told me not to worry,
It was just one of those things.
Bob Morton at the Big Sky Rodeo Company told me
The same thing happened to him,
In the same arena, in the same spot.
The boy who was killed was from Duncan, Arizona.
Pat Dolan was his name.
He won the bronc ridin' for the year,
Even though he was dead.
That spot is in the Northwest corner of the arena,
At Sixteen Hundred River Road, in Tucson.
People ask me, don't I mind fightin' bulls and rodeoin'?
I tell 'em I could be killed fallin' out of the bed.
I could be killed walkin' across a street.
I guess I'll do what I like.

—Voice of JAKE PAGE

The Gate

I stand here watching the light go by,
Like an old grey horse who stands in front of a gate
And watches the people go past,
And doesn't know a way to go through.

You take trails men have been riding
Through this border country for years.
Somebody comes and puts a fence across 'em.
I made my own gates, I did.

—Voice of WALTER RAMSEY

GUNS

Says Wiley Gatlin,
"The only pistol I'd ever have,
Is one with the front sight filed off.
Or one made of chocolate,
Then, when they told me to stuff it up my ass,
Or to eat it,
I'd be able to do what they said."

Range Country Wisdom

You take a good dog ...
He's got a purpose,
But if you don't give him nothin' to do ...
He'll go to killin' sheep.

Reminiscences

"Well I've been followin' cowboyin' now
For nearly fifty years," says Leo Turner.
"I've had some rough days.
I've had some pretty high-heeled times, too.
I've known a lot of men,
I've seen a lot of country,
I've made some good friends,
And I don't have any enemies.
They're all dead."

—Voice of LEO TURNER

• • • • •

TURQUOISE STONES IN THE CREEK BED ...
        THE SOUND OF THE HORSE'S HOOVES IN THE SAND.

History

Where Two Little Arroyos Come Together

Some years ago, there was a feller livin' over in Baker Canyon.
I don't know if he was the man
The canyon was named for, but he was livin' there.
Alvin Taylor's family homesteaded after him.
Our family homesteaded a little to the East of Alvin's.
There's still an old cookstove, and a few stove parts on the ground.
Anyway, the story we heard was,
A man came walkin' up Baker Canyon, and he had a gun.
The feller who was a-livin' in Baker had a dog.
Well, either the man who came up the canyon
Got bit by the dog, or thought he was a-goin' to get bit.
Anyway, he took up his gun and he shot the dog.
Well, that didn't go over too big, with the man who owned the dog.
The man who owned the dog up and shot the one who killed his dog.
The dog-killin' man is buried where two little arroyos come together up Baker,
But now, with all of the years and all of the rains, those winds and flash floods
That come down the canyon,
I guess that feller's bones are pretty well scattered.
Just yesterday evening, my dog brought me a bone.

—Voice of WALTER RAMSEY

Ready to Die with Your Boots On

"*Yo creo que no eres bastante hombre para matarme,*
   I don't think you are man enough to kill me," says the man.
"There are some problems it takes a funeral to cure," says Waylon.

Etiquette

   Juan Pedro came into the cantina.
   He put a quarter in the jukebox,
   Sat down to drink his beer.
   He wanted to hear an old Mexico tune.
   Another man came into the cantina,
   But the man didn't like Juan Pedro's selection.
   He pulled out the cord of the jukebox,
   Said he'd beat the shit out of Juan Pedro.
   Juan Pedro got up from the table.
   He went outside to his pickup truck.
   He walked back in with his .22 pistol.
   He sat down on the chair at the table.
   The other man pulled a knife.
   Juan shot the man in the side of the stomach.
"Now why the hell did you do that?"
   Mexico steer buyer Billy Brown asked Juan Pedro.
"*Siempre,* always," Juan Pedro exclaimed, smiling,
"When you take it out, you pull the trigger."

   —*Voices of* JUAN PEDRO *and Mexico steer buyer* BILLY BROWN

A Man's Word

Hoof and Mouth

During that hoof and mouth disease,
One of them border guards,
Who was a-ridin' for the Livestock Sanitary Board,
Came up to the ranch, up by Rodeo.
He told that rancher he was going to have to kill his cows.
He had on shiny boots and one of them expensive new hats.
I don't think there was a speck on it.
That old rancher told him not to kill his cows,
But that shiny-booted bastard did.
The old rancher took up his .30-.30 rifle
And shot that border guard right between the eyes.
"Yep," says Bill Bryan, "I guess he meant what he said."

—Voice of BRYAN RICE

Technology

A Colt .45 and a Chili Queen

I was camped at the Yerba Mansa,
When old Lee Howard rode into my camp one night.
He was headed into Mexico.
Told me he was goin' South to see his Chili Queen.
I was seventeen years old and kind of afraid of him,
But I had a Colt .45 he wanted.
He said I didn't need it and he probably would.
He kept a-stayin' there in my camp and a-stayin'.
Finally to get rid of him,
I let him trade me that grey mule for the Colt .45.
He decided to clean that gun by the campfire light.
Took it apart and lay the screws onto his saddle blanket.
All of a sudden, he heard a sound behind him.
He jumped up and his spur hung on the saddle blanket.
Well, the dust was three or four inches thick around him.
He may have found two or three screws, but that was all.
I come a-ridin' into camp the next day.
There was old Lee, whittlin' mesquite pegs
To put in the screw holes.
He told me, "When these old mesquite pegs get dry,
They'll be hard as iron."

—Voice of REX McDONALD

South of the Border

Gettin' Crossways

A few days later,
We were ropin' saddle horses out of the corral.
Him and my Uncle Davis got crossways.
Lee said, "I guess I'd better leave."
My uncle said, "I guess you'd better."
Lee gathered his camp outfit, packed his mule,
And rode away down the trail, just a-foggin' the dust.
But that mule didn't want to leave his pardner.
He broke in two and scattered Lee's gear all over the country.
I was horseback and headed the mule.
I hemmed him against a cliff.
Old Lee came ridin' up, a-cussin' and a-fumin',
Drew that Colt .45 out of its holster, and aimed it at the mule.
I sat there on my horse, watchin' what was goin' to happen.
"Hold it, hold it!" Lee said.
"I'm just a-gonna vaccinate that son of a bitch once and for all."
BOOM
The mule just stood there and flicked his ears a little.
Then I looked at old Lee.
He was standing with the handle of that Colt .45 in his hand,
The pieces scattered all over the ground around him.
I'd seen him try to shoot a man before,
'Cause the man didn't like the bread old Lee was making,
So I didn't laugh.
I gave him his mule back and he rode off,
South towards the Corral de Palos,
To go to see his Chili Queen.

—Voice of REX McDONALD

Skunks

Well, Lee Howard was a good feller,
Everybody liked him, but he was kind of dangerous.
He'd get mad at you and you didn't even know it.
Next thing he'd be a-shootin' at you.
One time, on a round-up,
The cowboys were camped over
At the U Bars North of Antelope Wells.
Lee woke in the middle of the night.
The night was hot and one of the
Mexican *vaqueros* had stuck a foot
Out of his bed roll.
The foot was shining in the moonlight.
Lee pulled his six-gun out from under his pillow
And shot that Mexican boy's toe off.
Of course, the boy woke up.
He asked Lee how come he done that?
Lee said he was sorry,
He thought the Mexican boy's foot
Was the white tail of a skunk,
Coming through the door
Just a-shining in that moonlight.
Old Lee, he was one more, that boy.

—Voice of WALTER RAMSEY

. . . . .

TURQUOISE STONES IN THE CREEK BED ...
            THE SOUND OF THE HORSE'S HOOVES IN THE SAND.

RUSTLERS

Hell, it was so quiet,
You could hear the moonlight a-shinin',
Burning calfhide in the dark.

Rasped Hooves

A Long Rope and a Wide Loop

John Valency was a pretty smart feller.
He was a fine hand with a horse too.
He could ride through a herd and sleeper more calves
Quicker and easier than any man I've ever seen.
He'd earmark 'em and another cowboy, ridin' through the herd,
Would see that cropped ear and think the calf was already branded.
John'd come back later to put his brand on the grown calf.
That was the style in them days.
Course, some men were just better at it than others,
But in those open range times,
Sometimes it was pretty hard to know just who owned a calf.
The custom was, that mavericks was fair game.
Everybody was a-doin' it, so it kind of evened out.

John used to ride down into Mexico.
He'd drive a few fat heifers back across the line.
He'd take 'em to a spring kind of hidden away,
Hide 'em in a rough canyon like Aquilas,
Then he'd brand 'em, and while he had 'em down,
He'd rasp their hooves nearly to the quick.
There was mighty few fences in this country in those days,
But with them rasped hooves,
Them heifers was as good as fenced in.
They'd stay there, near that spring,
till their hooves grew out and their brands peeled.
When they scattered out over the rangeland,
They'd be a-wearin' his brand.
It got so John couldn't hardly go down into Mexico no more,
'Cause them Mexicans knowed what he was a-doin'.
They woulda killed him, just like they killed Vivien Bass.
Yep, there's many a man got his start in these Borderlands,
A-packin' a long rope and a-swingin' a wide loop.

—Voice of ALVIN TAYLOR

Neighbors

Weaned

Well, on one of them big cow outfits,
It was pretty easy to kinda haze
A little homesteader's cow and calf off,
A long ways from the home ranch.
They'd wait till that momma cow
Kicked her calf off from a-suckin'.
Then they'd let the cow go back home alone.
Nobody knew what had happened to the calf.
When some of them big cow outfits was a-ranchin'
Out here in this Sulfur Springs Valley,
Them little homesteaders had to pack a long rope
And swing a wide loop just to stay even.
Forty years ago, somebody'd a-knowed better
Than to a-throwed your gate down on the ground,
Then turned them cattle onto another man's land.
Why, there'da been the goldarndest team ropin'
You ever saw in that oak and manzanita brush.
They'da done just like they done to the old Tombstone sheriff,
John Slaughter, when he pushed cattle in on 'em.
Why, them yearlings of Slaughter's was a-runnin'
Around the country a-wearin' tin cans on their tails,
Or somebody was a-ropin' one to put a tin can onto his tail,
That, or eat him.

—*Voice of* WALTER RAMSEY

Mavericks

"Walter, do you think there's enough wood for that branding fire?"
"How many calves you got?" says Walter.
"One," says Drum.
"Well, if you can't brand a calf with that much wood,
  You'll never make a rustler.
  Hell, I could brand a dozen with that much wood."
  Walter shows Drum how to lay the fire.
"And that's enough wood for a man to steal two calves.
  Now you don't want to make too big a fire," says Walter,
"And you don't want to make too much smoke,
  And you don't want to stay too long."
"Well, do these irons look ready?"
"I kind of doubt it. They brand better after dark anyway," says Walter.
"Now, if you want to make that brand look old,
  Put a wet gunnysack between the hide and the iron."
  Drum brings in the calf. "Well, is that a pretty good size?"
"Yeah, it sure is," says Walter. "One that size is
  Pretty easy broke away from his mammy.
  Them old big mavericks is like that,
  Why, anybody who's cowboy enough to catch one of 'em,
  Why, it's his."
  They whet their knives.
"Now a calf rustler don't go around with no dull knife neither," says Walter.
"You shoulda taught me better," says Drum.
"If I'da knowed you was gonna make a calf rustler,"
  Walter says, "I *woulda* taught you better."

—*Voice of* WALTER RAMSEY

The Preservation of Tradition

Fresh Meat for the Community

For some years, a neighbor had a few cows
Missing every Fall, at the end of the roundup time.
Fences weren't very good,
But after a number of years, he realized
That he had never gotten a cow back
From the other side of one of those leaky fences.
So, he preserved the old customs of the country.
He rustled a few cows from his neighbor.
He explained, "First you eat the calf, then you eat the cow."
After he did that, his own cows began to be returned,
From miles and miles, way off to the East,
Over the saddle on the cottonwood divide,
On the far side of that leaky preservation of tradition.
Cowboy logic, old-time custom,
Crooked neighbor's fallin' down fence.

—Voice of BILL McDONALD

BOOK TWO

· · · · ·

The
Mother
Lode

· · · · ·

TURQUOISE STONES IN THE CREEK BED ...
THE SOUND OF THE HORSE'S HOOVES IN THE SAND.

PREAMBLE

We are the last "first" people.

—CHARLES OLSON

The Borderlands was a time and a place
When men and women still knew
Where they came from and who they were,
And that milk came from off a cow
Instead of a supermarket, and meat
From the butchering of an animal.
They knew that under all the world's paved places
There was earth, even under the grasses and maple trees
In Central Park in New York City.
They knew their cars and trucks
And how to repair them with a pocket knife
Or a piece of their belts, or with wire
From a roadside fence, till 1970,
When all parts, even of washing machines,
Became plastic, televised, transistorized,
And had to be fixed by the specialists in the big cities,
With lost computerized souls, jailed within the walls
Of all human creations around them.

The Human Condition

Horseshoein'

Well, one day I was watchin' a feller.
He was havin' some trouble a-shoein' a horse,
But that feller, he always had his troubles shoein'.
I sat there and watched him a-wrastlin'
With that horse's hind leg and cussin' for a while.
I saw he was a-drivin' them horseshoe nails into the hoof
With the curved side pointed in instead of out.
He was a-hammerin' them nails in backwards!
Naturally, that horse was a-givin' him some trouble.
I sat there a little while longer and watched him some more.
Course, I didn't say nothin'.
I figured to myself if that feller was as old as he was,
And had cowboyed all of the years that he had,
And was still a-doin' it thatta way,
He just must notta wanted to know.

—Voice of WALTER RAMSEY

How to Read the Instructions

When I was young and hotheaded
I liked rodeoing around, but as I got older
I began to think maybe it was time to settle down.
I got a foreman job.
One day I was working cattle with a boy,
Cutting out cows and putting 'em through a gate.
He was guarding the gate.
Well, he turned seven or eight cows back over me.
I couldn't figure out if he was trying
To work me over or if he just didn't know.
That kid couldn't have poured piss out of a rubber boot
If the instructions was wrote on the heel.
I told him, "Listen, if you ain't gonna do anything else
With that horse, why don't you pull your saddle off
And take him to the barn and grain him and give him some hay?"
Well, goddamn, that's just what he done.
He took his horse to the stall and pulled his saddle off
And grained him and went to town.
He wasn't trying to work me over.
The poor kid just didn't know.

—Voice of LEE ROBBINS

How the Earth Mixes the Trail

Nadie Nace Enseñado

"No one is born knowing."
First you've got to know the dust,
The sunlight and the wind.
They mix the trail you follow.
Then you've got to watch the morning frost
Come and go, and change the print of a foot on the earth.
Then you've got to follow the tracks of blood and flesh,
How a cow tends to swing her head towards that place,
Her *querencia*, where she wants to go.
How a lion doubles back over his track,
To sit on a cliff above the dogs,
To watch the lion hounds pass him by.
How a man's work changes the look of his face.
How a voice tells where a man's been.
All you've got to do is ride through these canyons
And the mountains here, to listen
And watch the earth going by you,
For about forty years.

—Voice of MARVIN GLENN

Words and the Wind

These poems will go with the wind,
To blow along the slopes of blue mountain ranges,
Changing here, turning there,
Because words in the wind are all I know.

Rhymes

Springtime was here fifty-five thousand years ago,
Shadows playing in this old arroyo bed.
Blond hair, antelope, light blue eyes
Covered by pages of blowing sands and time.
Fought and loved, lay down and died.
Seeds blooming, shadows playing,
Old fossil blood crooning, casting these rhymes.

VOICES OF THE RANGELANDS

This world is a great place to live,
But there are sure some pretty sorry SOBs in it.
So the value of the world changes,
As the SOBs increase and decrease.

—Voice of OLD MAN BEN WILLIAMS

. . . . .

TURQUOISE STONES IN THE CREEK BED ...
        THE SOUND OF THE HORSE'S HOOVES IN THE SAND.

Bill Bryan

Small hands, greying hair,
The light blue laughter of his eyes.
A Bible and an ashtray on the chair by his bed.
The skin of his hands wrinkled
And puffed with the smoking of cigarettes.
He sits on the wood chair
To look out the kitchen window.
He was a drifting cowboy,
Bronc and bull rider on the rodeo circuit,
Then ranch manager, then ranch owner.
Now, an aged cowboy remembering
What was the American Southwest.
"When I was young, it didn't matter
To me how much a horse bucked.
After the first few jumps
I'd jest raise up offa the ground
On my elbow 'n' watch 'im.
They used to pack me
Into the Bradshaw Mountains in early Summer.
They'd leave me there with gentle horses,
They'd come a-lookin' fer me in the Fall.
I was worried that I wouldn't git enough
Of them wild yearlings gathered
To make the boss think I'd worked all Summer long.
I'd rope 'em, tie 'em, and brand 'em
Where I found 'em.
That old horse, Patches, I reckon he's kinda like me.
He stays by himself in that Stony Lonesome Pasture."

The Law

Goin' to Jail

Well, I guess I'm a-goin' to jail.
They keep sendin' me these government cattle census reports.
They tell me it's law number so and so. I got to fill 'em out.
I guess I'm a-goin' to jail, 'cause I just throw 'em into the wastebasket.
There's already been two phone calls while I was at the ranch.
I don't know how many while I wasn't.
A nice girl called to ask how I could keep on ranchin'
Without the information in those cattle census reports.
I told her I didn't know,
But I'd been doin' it somehow, for the past thirty years.
I told her those cattle reports didn't mean too much,
'Cause nobody ever wrote down anythin' that was true in 'em anyway.
Why, if the cattle census taker, the banker, and the tax man
Ever got together in the same room,
We'd all be out of business.
'Course those cattle census reports
Never include the Summer nor Winter rains neither.
She said then, "Just what do you base your business decisions on?"
I told her, "What I got between my ears."
I told her it wasn't much.
I told her it was wrong about ninety percent of the time,
But at least it was mine.
She thanked me and hung up.

—Voice of BILL BRYAN

An Open Mind

An Old Cowboy and Barbwire

Well, Drum wanted to build a fence like people have been doin'
For the last fifty years or so,
To keep cows from grubbin' out a softer part of the pasture
And make 'em start grazin' more on the mountain sides,
Where there was a lot of water and good grass feed.
"Walter," Drum says to his old friend, who was raised
On a part of this outfit about seventy years ago,
"Let's go see where we could run a fence line through the deer track's pasture.
I'd sure appreciate it if you'd tell me where you think it oughta go."
They mount up and ride a while,
And get to where Drum thought the fence should be.
Walter sets there on his horse, looks around.
"Drum," he finally says, after a long time.
"An old cow is kinda like a human.
If she don't like a country, she ain't a-gonna stay there.
In a pasture that's big and open like this, she can go and come
When she wants, and roam around free.
Barbwire. Barbwire is what's ruined all this land.
Ruined what was big and open and cow country.
If this was my ranch, I wouldn't build a fence on it.
Still, if you're set to build it,
We'll flag it out with mescal stalks.
Set 'em in piles of rocks,
A fence here might not hurt *too* much,
And it might do *some* good.
C'mon, let's go."

—*Voice of* WALTER RAMSEY

By the Maidenhair Fern Springs

I.

    A spirit beside my body passing along a trail,
    Greasewood and ocotillo blowing in the wind,
    A fly buzzing, soft on the soft salt earth.
    Time after time, we tie the stays to the wire,
    The darkness of our shadows
    Falling to the pebbles and sand on the ground.
    Cows grazing on a grey ridge to the North,
    The stems of our darknesses open and close
    Like seeds lying on the ground before the rains.

II.

    Golden webs spun across the trail,
    Riding East into the sun,
    A grasshopper, caught on the barbwire,
    And everywhere I look for them.
    The wind is blowing the seeds of black grama,
    And a cow bawling in the distance.
    The horse pulls his reins against my hand,
    And we move on across the flats.

III.

    The sun floating like the moon behind grey clouds,
    Towns spread out along the arroyos,
    The arroyos washing through the land.
    The grass is green under the junipers,
    The calves are ready for shipping.
    When will she come home?

IV.

    The years seem as though nothing were in them,
    Passing along the West side of Leslie Canyon,
    The road blasted into the rock and up across the divide,
    The wind blowing down towards Douglas.

A Song of Crickets

I'll sing you a song about the goddamn crickets,
While we sit here by the pale arroyo sands,
As though you'd want to know ...
All there is, that a cricket could sing,
While the poor wills whistle back and forth, calling in slow time,
Through white patches in the moonlight
Twoo twoou ... twoo twoou ... twoo twoou.
When we're old and then gone, the cricket's song says,
And the young Earth lies here still,
Playing by the canyon tanks in Guadalupe, in April,
You'll hear the beginning of Springtime come up from Mexico,
When the wind begins to blow first cool,
Then warm on the backs of your hands,
When you ride a colt along these ridges in the morning.
And the years and those winds will slow, and then go past,
Growing, and drying out the seeds and your heart, and the grasses ...
In the dusk and these blue distances, you can hear them come, and go,
As though in that rippled slow sound of their singing,
Some other old song called from here to you,
Back and forth, in slow time through the moonlight.
Tongues from some old heart, songs of hearts that played awhile,
Came and played awhile, till they were done and sung away.
Whirling old Earth, come gather me these songs in the moonlight,
Under the canyon rim in Guadalupe.
I hear the crickets and the poor wills singing.
Hear them while these Spring times go drifting away,
Twoo twoou ... twoo twoou ... twoo twoou.
But really, I never could figure out
What those darn crickets were saying.
"Well, one thing's for sure," says Bud Robbins "Whatever it is,
They sure keep a-sayin' it over, and over, and over again ..."

—Voice of BUD ROBBINS

A Cowboy

Gone Riding

Old Walter Ramsey, he's another lost lover.
The years and the winds have played like a woman's light hands,
Along the corners of his eyes, the dry lines of his skin.
So he knows those light, shifting moods
That sunlight and rainwater and drifting winds bring,
While he's easing slowly along the canyons.
In Summer, he's following the shade around a sycamore tree.
In Winter, maybe riding by the ridgeline trail across the snow.
Sunlight and Springtime, shadows and blowing leaves ...
Old Walter, trailing the light years through these mountain passes,
Where have you gone riding, where do those tracks go?

A Bulldozer Poem

Ode to a Caterpillar

Goddamn I'm gonna tell you a bulldozer poem.
Hijo de la chingada, these tracks go around,
Like the wailin' in my heart when my soul's run aground.
Shit hit that rock too hard, clackin' along,
To nowhere too soon.
Juniper needles down the back of my neck,
Runnin' along in second gear low range
Is too much for this old trail.
Walter and the *mojados* been waitin' two days,
Up by the Valenci Draw,
Comin' along behind. Berto's bringin' along the mesquite grubber,
Chuggin' along with four-wheel drive.
How are we gonna get that half ton mesquite grubber out
Of the bed of the pickup truck and onto the blade of the dozer?
Hell, we'll hoist it
From a limb of one of these black jack oaks.
"Now you're fixin' to tear down my trees."
Walter says, "I might push
Some old widow woman's ducks in the creek someday,
And need to hide out under the limbs of these old black jack oaks."
"Just what do you mean, Walter,
Push some old widow woman's ducks in the creek someday?"
"Well, Drum, at my age,
That's about the worst thing I could do to her."

—Voice of WALTER RAMSEY

THE HOMESTEADERS

Nicknames of the first settlers ...
Duck on the Hill,
Old Lady Baconrind,
Hollow Eye,
Palomino,
Chief,
Half-face,
Pretty Boy,
Snow Shoes,
Battleship, Shrivel Prick,
No Chin.

• • • • •

TURQUOISE STONES IN THE CREEK BED ...
            THE SOUND OF THE HORSE'S HOOVES IN THE SAND.

Old Ways

"I'll tell you about the first people who came to stay.
It's how the borderland was settled," says Walter.
"It may take some time for your head
To understand these stories.
They were from that frontier world when
A man had to think in a different way to stay alive.
Cada cabeza es un mundo, each head is a world,"
Walter quotes the Mexican *dicho*.
"But we had worlds of time and a stillness for thinking too.
We were herders in a big open country.
There wasn't a fence for twenty-five miles
From the Puerta Blanca to Antelope Wells."

—Voice of WALTER RAMSEY

John Connell's Ax

John's got an ax with a handle that's curved as a snake.
The snake curve in the handle throws off
Where your eyes tell you the target is.
You got to aim for someplace else
To put the damn thing near where you want it.
Summers and Winters of chopping this piñon and cedar
For a family that's come to live in an adobe house,
On the side of the ridge where the Tusas Creek
Runs out of the pools in the gorge
And begins to ease into the Petaca Valley.
Curves in the ax handle, curves in your shoulders,
Curves in your spine, curves in your legs,
Curves in the ridges, in the earth you're born with,
Flecks in the cedar bark and piñon logs in front of you.
How the hell are you gonna chop that wood?
Damned if I know how, but he did it.

Women of the West

The Hired Gunman and Old Lady Cosper

Well Bill Hennessy, he done some cowboyin',
But he was mostly kind of a hired gun for John Slaughter.
One day, Slaughter asks him to go on up to Cottonwood Canyon,
To run off the Cosper family who were homesteadin' there.
Bill Hennessy catches a horse, saddles up.
He rides over to Cottonwood Canyon.
He goes to the adobe house, knocks on the door.
Old Lady Cosper comes to the door, opens it just a crack.
"Mrs. Cosper," says Bill Hennessy, "I'm sorry,
But Mr. Slaughter told me to talk to you folks.
This is his range. You've got to move on."
Old Lady Cosper reaches behind the door.
She comes up with a .30-.30 Winchester rifle.
She points it at Bill Hennessy and says, through the crack,
"I'll give you just five minutes to get
Down around that thar bend."
"I think I give her back three of those five minutes,"
Says Bill Hennessy, when he rides back to Slaughter's.
"That old lady's crazy.
She's a-gonna kill somebody one of these days."

—Voices of BILL HENNESSY *and* WALTER RAMSEY

Sarah Bennet

Our roots were tugged up so many times,
I guess we were like them tumbleweeds,
When the last part of the root dries up,
And goes blowin' across all of that country,
From Texas to Arizona.
Poppa was part Texas Indian.
He said there used to be women who were warriors.
There still are.
It's just sometimes, men forget what they know.
But, if he hadn't a-told us that, we couldn't a-come all that way,
A-hangin' by the shred of a root, sometimes.
We'd stop for the night,
Rolled up against a cliff
That gave us a little protection from the wind.
Or we'd stop when we found a waterin' hole for our stock.
If we saw a bottle or a can by the side of the trail,
We always had a use for it.
A twist of wire around the top and the bottom of a can,
Would make a coffee cup.
When we girls were young, Poppa would say,
"Bloom where you're planted."
I guess we were planted all along that way across the mesas,
The blue valleys, and mountains from Texas to Arizona.
All of us would try to stay, put down roots,
Raise a family by a seep spring up a canyon,
Out of the wind with an arroyo tricklin' through,
And a lone cottonwood or two,
To tell that the water would be there for us.
But then'd come a few dry years.
We'd find ourselves droughted out, rooted up,
Lookin' for another canyon with a cottonwood, or a big sycamore,
A spring, that could give us water, and be a home.

The Coming and the Going

Ida Page

My mother come here from Texas.
She liked to fish and she liked to shoot squirrels.
In them days, we had no radio, no icebox,
No telephone, no bathroom except a privy.
But we always got by.
We used to ride horseback thirty miles to go to a dance.
We didn't live on anything, we just lived.
There's been such a change in people then and now.
In them days, a man might kill you,
But if he told you he'd pay you
At a certain time, he would.
In those days a man gave you his word,
And in those days, a man's word was good.
My daddy was James R. Miller.
He filed on his homestead
By two walnut trees right there in Rodeo.
He lived there till he died.
My daddy used to say "One day
You're a bloomin' rose,
The next day you're gone."
I'm ninety-two years old,
I guess some day pretty soon
In the middle of the day one day,
I'll still be here just a-bloomin'
Till that next day when I'll be gone.

Agriculture

At sixteen, Ishmael Fairchild came from Texas in a wagon to the Borderland. Squarely built, so stout if he got a hold on the saddle horn, no bronc could throw him, so stout he never lost a fight against another man. "But to win," he said, "a man had to be ready to last at least an hour."

Rolling the Dice Farming

"Sunshine and me," says Ishmael Fairchild,
"We had about six hundred acres up by Elfrida.
We were bringin' in about seventy thousand dollars a year,
Then I got mercury poisonin' and couldn't work.
We started losin' about twenty thousand dollars a year.
The bank hornswoggled us out of that farm.
We lost it all, but what the heck, if we'd made it,
We just woulda wished we'd made more anyway.
Farmin' is kinda like prospectin'.
It's kinda like rollin' the dice.
It's somethin' you're a-lookin' for,
That the chances are pretty good,
You ain't a-gonna find.
I've seen fellers go out and think they're a-gonna find it.
And after ten or fifteen years, they still haven't got nothin'.
You'da thought they'da got discouraged, a-follerin' it,
But some of 'em, they just go right ahead.
They foller it, for all the rest of their lives."

Hope

A Well in the Desert Country

Six hundred feet
$66.66 a foot
$3,999.00
Dry as a popcorn fart

Goat Ranchers

By Yonder Ridgeline

They'd come up the arroyo road to their old homestead,
Where they lived when they were married those fifty years ago.
"You sure been married a long time," Drum says.
"It's like yesterday," says Ishmael. "It goes by like nothin'.
But Sunshine, she was wild then.
She used to ride this dirt road a-horseback.
She'd jump right over these cattle guards here."
They walked off,
Went all over the canyons and ridgelines.
Went where they'd herded goats when they were kids,
Went where they were lovers,
Went where they were married here, those fifty years ago.
Traces of Ishmael's ax on the scarred trunks of the cedar trees,
Crossing the canyons and winding arroyos.
One wheel of their daughter's baby carriage
Still lies in the leaves by their old homestead,
A mound of adobe bricks melting onto the rocky ground.
They ran a herd of five hundred angora goats all over the ridges.
Sunshine and Ishmael slept with them at night,
To keep the lions and the bobcats from carrying them away.
Our paths cross again later in the day, by the edge of the shadows,
Drifting along the canyon road, under the cottonwood leaves.
"Sunshine found a coffee pot a hangin' on the pasture fence post,
Way off by yonder ridgeline," says Ishmael.
"She packed it all the way back here to the canyon."
"I'll take it home to put a bird's nest in it.
I'll hang it from the eaves of our roof," says Sunshine.
They disappear, walking along the dusty arroyo road,
Old shadows drifting away between the patches of sunlight,
Mixing with the light wind in the cottonwood leaves,
Sunshine, and Ishmael, and a coffee pot.

—Voices of SUNSHINE *and* ISHMAEL

It Doesn't Really Matter

A Mexican Homesteader and a Straddlejack Fence

Skin stained brown, then browner by the sun
A white band, the shadow from his sombrero
In the wrinkled skin above his forehead,
His belly just beginning to push
Over the edge of his worn belt buckle.
The prints of his footsteps turned outward in the dust.

"Juan," I say to my steady Mexican ranch hand,
  When he's about to go home, Christmastime of 1978,
"It doesn't matter how long you stay home,
  But I'll need to know a day when you'll be back,
  So Carlos and Roberto can come at the same time
  And we can all get to work on that Escondida fence.
  We'll have to do it in the Winter because that's the only time
  There'll be drinking water enough in those potholes
  To let us pack in our camp and stay there.
  It's too far to ride all the way over there every day."
"I'll be back here January eighth," Juan says.
Well, Eastertime rolls around and old Juan still isn't back yet.
It doesn't really matter, 'cause Carlos and Roberto
Never have been at the ranch at the same time either.
And there's been so much snow and rain, there wouldn't have been
Enough dry dirt to make the fence posts hold anyway.
Ah, I forgot. Dry dirt wouldn't have mattered much, 'cause most of that fence
Will have to be a straddlejack fence, built over solid bedrock and cliffs.
I begin to think maybe Juan has built some of those kind of fences before.
I begin to wonder if maybe Juan meant next January of 1980.

September 13, 1979

Mañana

There is Old Juan standing in the middle of the corral laughing,
"¿Qué tal, Juan? ¿Cómo estás? What brings you here?"
"Pues, un viento del norte me trajo y me dejó aquí.
Well a wind from the North brought me and dropped me here," he says.
"And a wind from the South carried you to Summer in Northern Arizona, I guess?"
"Sí," he says. "I'm learning to ride those winds. I'm getting old.
When my time comes, I'll just hitch on to the wind and drift
Towards whatever way seems best at the time,
Heaven or the other way."
That old Juan, he's spent fifty years drifting,
Past mountain ranges, and windmills, and horses, and cows, and fence lines.
He may stay circling in one place for a while,
Like the rains that will be good help to you for maybe a year or two,
But he's like the changing Earth. He comes with his winds and stories
Laughing down the Valenci ridge. But if anyone wants to know
Good ranches to work between Northern Arizona and Old Mexico,
Or whose footprints, with the toes turned outward just a little,
Are crossing before him by the borderline,
Or whose woman is sleeping with Carlos Ramos,
Or where the last smuggler's trail goes,
Just ask old Juan. As if he'd tell you what he knows.
He's seen the wet years and the dry years
Come through these desert rangelands and go.
That old Juan, he's followed his winds. That old Juan, he knows
Not to come back to Guadalupe to build a straddlejack fence.

—Voice of JUAN

Demography

Too Close to Home

"Who homesteaded this ranch first?"
 Says wild Bill Remington.
"Lee Hudspath," Drum says,
"He had a pretty good outfit started.
 Had a house, a spring, a horse pasture.
 Then the Law got to trompin' too close on his tail.
 He skipped out, left it all, went to South America."
"Yep, I sure understand," says Bill.
"Killed someone too close to home."

SETTLING OF THE BORDERLANDS

Walter walks up to a crumbling slab of cement.
"This was where our fireplace was," he says.
"When we lived here, under this oak tree,
We never did go to town more than twice a year."

—Voice of WALTER RAMSEY, *West of the Blair Windmill*

• • • • •

TURQUOISE STONES IN THE CREEK BED ...
THE SOUND OF THE HORSE'S HOOVES IN THE SAND.

Geological Time

One Old Friend Remembering Another

"I used to see Roy Boss pretty often around town," says Walter,

"But you don't see him much since he's got married."
  Having lived around old Walter for the last seven years or so,
  Drum begins to suspect something.
"Well, just when did he get married?" says Drum.
  Old Walter thinks a moment,
  Rests his chin on his hand and grins,
"Oh, maybe forty years ago."

—Voice of WALTER RAMSEY

Migration

A Case of Mistaken Identity in the
Big Bend Country of West Texas

"My Uncle Roy got shot at here twice," Bill Bryan says,
"Comin' up Limpia Creek Canyon,
  But it was a case of mistaken identity.
  Hell, if that son of a bitch coulda shot straight,
  It woulda been all the same.
  The feller yelled to Uncle Roy,
'Hey aren't you so and so?'
  Uncle Roy yelled back, 'Heck no.'
'Oh, sorry, I didn't think so,' the man said,
  And went off ridin' down the canyon."

—Voice of BILL BRYAN

Innovation

A Meeting of the Cultures

Roberto Ávilez, my fine, *mojado* Mexican cowboy
Who's been on the trail for months and months,
And who's ridden hundreds and hundreds of miles,
Who can rope and tie down a wild Brahma bull,
Is cleaning out the goat's ear
With the nozzle of an air compressor.

• • • • •

There is Porfirio, El Güero, the white one, thin mustache, dignified, greying. Of Spanish blood, sits very straight in the saddle, square handsome chin. He tells when the rain will come by looking at the tipped points of the new moon. When Porfirio walks into the bunkhouse, and sits by the old woodstove in the stillness of the adobe room, his sombrero is muy agachado, *pulled down low, and he doesn't say anything, but bends his head, eyes turned away, looking at nothing, there, by his left shoulder. "Then," says María, "él anda con la luna, he is with the moon again. All of his family say it is true."*

Porfirio's Song

When you've lost touch
With the sound of your own voice, he takes your pain away.
Your own voice knew once how to take the pain away,
As the sound of a strumming guitar,
While you lie on your back aching
In an old adobe room
Where you see the windows broken,
When the evening light comes in
And makes the pale glass cobweb white.
There, Porfirio strums the guitar and takes your pain away,
While your heart follows the rhythm of his song,
Instead of the throbbing pain.

A Calf with Three Legs

One day, Porfirio and Drum were riding together
They came upon a young calf
Who had been born with only three legs.
The calf's right front leg was missing.
Porfirio looked at the calf for a long time.
Finally, he said, *"La luna le comió la pierna, digo yo,*
the moon ate the leg, say I."

—*Voice of* PORFIRIO

Anthropology

Regionalism

Mexican homesteader Porfirio and his friend, Roberto,
Had come to Agua Prieta,
From the San Bernardino Valley in Sonora,
Where Porfirio had spent nearly all of his life.
They were drinking tequila in a cantina.
They were sitting next to some *viejas,*
Some girls, one with a big stomach.
Roberto asked her what happened to her stomach.
"Un cabrón en Chihuahua me agarró y me culió.
One of those bastards in Chihuahua
Got ahold of me and got me," she said.
"Fíjate,
Imagine that," said Porfirio,
"They do it over there in Chihuahua, too."

—*Voices of* ROBERTO *and* PORFIRIO

• • • • •

They knew only their place,
And *"El lado donde se sube el sol,*
The side of the Earth
Where the sun comes up,
Y el lado donde se mete el sol,
And the side of the Earth where the sun goes away."
And to be *norteado,* to be "Northed,"
Meant that one was lost.

Gold

The Mother Lode

Take those first men and women,
A-comin' through these mountain ranges—
All they knew was a wagon and a team,
And a little camp outfit in their wagon.
They might notta gone two miles in a day.
And, when night overtook 'em,
They stopped right there where they were.
They hobbled their mules,
And them mules could get a bellyful
On any one of these mountainsides.
I never found much gold when I rode
Down there in them Sierra Madres,
A-prowlin' with a pack horse.
I was always too busy a-lookin'
For what was over that next ridge.
But one time, I went down there deer huntin'.
I was prospectin' too, of course.
Me and my horse crossed a rough, brushy canyon.
It was about ten miles South of the Lang Camp.
It was in June, just before the start of the Summer rains.
That canyon still had a little water
A-tricklin' through it in the rock pools.
I was thirsty. I stepped down offa my horse to get a drink.
When I put my face close to the pool,
You know, like a man will, to see what's there,
To blow the water clear before his lips touch it,
I looked and saw a dark streak on the bottom of the pool.
It had flecks of a gold color.
It run off into the cliff rock.
Well I set there on that warm sand, a-lookin' at them colors.
I was a-thinkin' about old Jim Hewlet,
When he made his strike in the Tigre Mountains.
He staked his claim,
Then he took two engineers out there to look at it.
One said, "It's just surface gold on this rock ledge.

It ain't a mine; it won't go down."
But the other one broke a chunk off,
Looked at it a while, and he said,
"It is a mine and it's a good one and it'll go down."
It went down two hundred feet and turned out just like he said.
His company give Jim five hundred thousand dollars for the claim.
But the money didn't do old Jim no good,
For he was hell to gamble.
He bought a saloon in Agua Prieta.
He had a gamin' table runnin' most alla the time.
That money pretty quick was gone.
Jim and me prospected together in them Sierra Madres a long time,
That's how he told it to me.
Well I set there, on that warm sand,
I watched the water a-tricklin'.
I was camped to the North by a seep spring,
Where a man mighta found water
Even in the driest time a the year,
That is, by diggin' down on it.
I rode to my camp where I'd left my prospect pick.
I come back to that pool where I'd seen the gold colors.
I broke off quite a little sample to have it assayed.
It wasn't high, but it wasn't low.
It was when gold was thirty-five dollars an ounce.
It was when silver was seventy cents.
Stewart Hunt reckoned I should take a diamond drill in there,
But hell, I didn't have that kind of money.
The ledge of ore crossed the canyon.
It disappeared into those mountain cliff rocks.
It was just a little stringer of ore in a rock pool I drank from,
But if a man coulda managed to follow it,
It mighta led him right into the mother lode.

—Voice of WALTER RAMSEY

. . . . .

Anybody who's got enough money to mine,
Doesn't need to mine.
A miner is a liar with a hole in the ground.
It's just as well to lose it quickly,
'Cause then you can go home and rest.
The quicker you mine it, the quicker you lose it.

—*Voice of* OLD MAN BEN WILLIAMS

The Tracks of Civilization

Till about 1939 or '40, we had only carbide lights.
When a man goes into a drift to get the ore,
Sometimes he feels the earth begin to move.
He sees the air around him begin to fill with fine dust,
And the particles of dust get to be like pebbles,
And the timber starts to crack like the the sounds like a gun,
Then he stands holding his pinch bar,
He listens in the quiet to the sounds of the cracking timber
Coming closer and closer. Then he can hear his heart beat.
Bisbee ore was hard. Most levels were one hundred feet apart.
A man drives up to a drift or crosscut.
There is a lot of powder shot and a lot of drilling done.
If a man is working a lead and he leaves,
And the lead has caved in, then he may need to shoot with water.
A friend of mine opened a door and hit a pocket of water.
The water mixed with the falling earth and began to bury him.
I found him and gave him mouth to mouth
But I couldn't bring him back.
Another friend stood in a crosscut
When a boulder came from his right side.
He was knocked down. I started moving towards him.
But when I got to him he was already gone.
There is a green copper water that comes from the ore.
If it touches a man's eyes, he will think that he is going blind.

In a stope in a lead end there is a big blower
To bring in the fresh air. If the blower quits ...
Get the hell out if you can.
I was standing next to my brother when he went
From the manway ten feet up into a stope after the blower quit ...
He turned to pick up a tool ...
There's ground that will give off oxygen.
There's ground that won't.
Sometimes a man will slowly go down on his knees
To the ore car tracks. It looks as if he is praying,
Then his body and his choking lungs
Will try to give strength to his hand, to follow the ore car rail
Until he can come to the fresh air.
My brother never got to the fresh air.
They say silver is industrial, gold is exotic.
In Mexico, Old Man Cayatano was pinching gold and silver.
It used to be three weeks to get the ore to the smelter on burros in 1916.
No había ni vereda, there was not even a trail.
Sometimes a shot round of the dynamite doesn't break.
The unbroken round is called a skinner.
If a miner drills into a skinner, it is the only mistake he will ever make.
In the oxide zone, everything has been leeched out.
I sit here in this barroom and look at the brands on the walls
And study the newspapers and the people passing.
I remember my brother who never made it back to the air.
In the last ten years, in the world of electronics,
We have used two billion ounces of silver.
All that is left now are the stains of everything that's gone.

—Voice of ED McDONALD

TOWN

I'm gonna get married if I can make a livin'," says Regin Taylor.
"Regin," says Dan Taylor, "what are you talkin' about makin' a livin' for?
I could sit on a rock an' make a livin'."
Two years later when Regin is out of a job, he says,
"I'd sure like to find that rock you been sittin' on."

A Rich Mexico Rancher Comes to Town

From across the Line to Do a Little Gallivantin' in the Gadsden Hotel, the B & P Bar, and Other Douglas Gringo Oases

"Well," Puyo says, after he and the boys had quenched their thirst
With a few *raspabuches,* gizzard scratchers,
And were feelin' pretty good and about ready to go back home to Mexico,
But they needed the car they'd come in.
"Well," Puyo says, "I guess I'm not settin' a very good example for you boys.
We've lost the darn car.
Oh what the hell, it was only a goddamn Chevrolet. Call a taxi."

Water-Witching in the Gadsden Barroom

"It's something a man or a woman has got deep down
In the subconscious, telling where the stream runs,"
Pete Middleton says. "I guess witching lets it out.
Double, double, toil and trouble, cauldron seethe…
I know a bank where the wild heather grows…
I know a stream of water that flows under the Gadsden Barroom.
It runs at one hundred and ten feet.
The other night I witched it over by the juke box.
It goes past the two pool tables on the North side of the bar,
Runs across the dance floor through the beer drinking tables,
Then swerves a little towards the women's room
But unfortunately goes into the men's."
We drink to it with a bottle of beer.
Nobody knows where it goes from here,
Nobody cares, but it's good to know there's another stream
That runs deep down in the earth under
The concrete floor of the Gadsden Barroom.
But as Pete says, "Filtered through a few kidneys,
It all disappears."

> —*Voice of* PETE MIDDLETON, *Australian mercenary soldier,*
> *fighter pilot in the Second World War,*
> *bomber pilot in Korea, helicopter pilot in Vietnam.*

Adentro

"Do you want a drink?" asks Ben.
"Well," says his friend, "I really don't like
To have a drink until later in the day."
"Well," says Ben, "Do you know when
I've found is a good time to have a drink,
Is when you want one."

Dame un traguito. Mi corazón me lo pide.
Give me a little drink. My heart tells me to ask you.
Hermoso líquido, dulce tormento,
Ven conmigo, vamos adentro.
Beautiful liquid, sweet torment,
Come with me now, let's go inside.

A Gizzard Scratcher

To Quench a Man's Thirst

Well Stan Hall is kind of a polite, quiet man,
A fine cowboy, with a good steady job, a wife, and three good kids.
But every now and then, he goes to town to quench his thirst
With a few gizzard scratchers in the B & P and the Mexico cantina bars.
Finally, he starts talking, gets to fighting,
The police on his trail from one broken-up cantina bar to another,
Old Stan was staying just ahead of the *policía,*
Then they open the door of that cantina where he is, and they've got him.
After one more pretty good battle, there he lays in the *calabozo* jail.
They usually let him out the next day.
He takes just one more drink for the road,
Maybe turns over his truck, runs into a cow or two,
But he makes it home safe.
"I hear you left a pretty good trail in town a week or so ago."
"Yep," Stan says, looking kind of wistful into the distances,
Shifts his weight, heaves a sigh,
"I don't know why I did all that,
But it sure seemed like the right thing to do at the time."

—Voice of STAN HALL

Some Exceptions

"Howdy, howdy," says old Lee Burnett.
"How's things at your ranch?
  It's rained so much at my place,
  The buzzards are afraid to fly over,
  'Fraid they'll get their flappin' shadows bogged.
  All a rainy day is fit for
  Is drinkin' beer, playin' poker, or makin' love.
  As few rainy days as we've got in Cochise County, Arizona,
  There's no goddamn sense in wastin' 'em workin'.
  I've given up huntin' a good woman, wives are easier to find.
  You know," says old Lee,
"I quit drinkin' for about the last two months. I made a big discovery.
  I found out that the majority of the assholes that you run around with
  When you are drinkin', are some of the sorriest bastards
  That you ever knew when you're sober.
  There are some exceptions of course, like you and me.
  Those bastards, they'll take your last penny for their last drink
  When you've been out drinkin' with 'em all night.
  They really don't give a damn whether you get home alive or dead.
  Those are some of my dear friends when I've been drinkin'.
  There are some exceptions of course, like you and me."

—*Voice of* LEE BURNETT

The B & P Palace

The Pool Game

Boots, Levi's, silver belt buckle, blue striped shirt,
Dark tan face, soft and hard, scarred by bulls and horses.
Nose that's been broken, bent a little to one side,
Staggering softly around the green pool table.
"I'll lay you a quarter on this game I beat you,"
He says to another cowboy,
"So I'll know you don't give it to me if I win."
Five balls left for him to sink and one for the other cowboy.
Click, click, the pool balls roll.
Outside he says, "That son of a bitch laughin' at me
Was my brother-in-law's brother.
I don't mind losin', but I don't like
That son of a bitch laughin' at me.
I think I'll go on back in there
To mash his face in the ground."
Click, click, the pool balls roll.
"I'll lay you another quarter on this game
So I'll know you didn't give it to me
If I beat you and win,"
He says again to the other cowboy.
He finishes his tequila and goes back outside.
"He may a whipped me again,
But I think I oughta mash his face in the ground."

"Some men are like a-shootin' stars," says the bartender.
"They burn pretty bright till they flame out."

—Voice of WALTER HUNT

Tryin' to Figure

People Watchin'

"I study people a lot," says old Ed McDonald,
  Bisbee miner for thirty-five years.
"But I study my wife most.
  Course that's 'cause she's right in front of me.
  I'll look at her and be a-tryin' to figure her out.
  'Is there somethin' wrong?' I'll say to her.
  'Well, why do you think there's something wrong?' she'll say.
  'Well, it's just kind of the way you look.'
  'What do you mean, don't I look all right?' she says.
  'No, it ain't that,' I'll say.
  'I just thought maybe you was sick or somethin'.'
  Well, that about ends it 'cause we don't say nothin'
  To each other for three or four hours after that.
  Maybe I don't have a lot to do. Maybe I'll get to watchin' TV.
  You know it sure gets on a woman's nerves
  When she sees you just settin' around, watchin' TV.
  These women, they wash dishes and go shoppin'.
  They keep movin' all the time.
  But you know maybe that's how come
  They live so much longer than us men.
  Well, I'll be a-watchin' her and she'll say,
  'When are you gonna get up and do somethin'?'
  And I'll say, 'What the hell, I'm retired.'
  Then she'll say, 'You worked for Phelps Dodge, and you retired.
  I been workin' for you and the kids all my life,
  Nobody never give me no retirement check.
  I don't see you got a right to be layin' around,
  When I'm not layin' around.'
  About then, I take the dog and go to the cemetery for a walk,
  Or I go out to my shop.
  But I'll guarantee you can't out-guess a woman ...
  Pretty soon she comes there a-huntin' me.
  'Why are you sleepin' out here on this bench?' she'll ask me.

'Oh, the noise ain't so bad,' I'll say.
'What do you mean, what kind of noise?' she'll say.
'Oh, maybe the TV,' I say.
So I go out and watch the people,
And listen to 'em talk about this integration
Or whatever else that's news.
These damn Okies and Texicans, hell,
They'll sleep with them colored girls at night,
But they won't ride the bus with 'em in the day.
A feller said, 'You white folks been foolin' around so much
With Mexicans and colored people.
Nobody can tell who the hell they are any more.'"

Changin' clouds, turnin' Earth,
All of it passin' till our days are done.
And we old fools sittin' watchin'
These years, our wives, the sunlight, the people passin' by.

A No Parkin' Zone

The Settling of Bisbee, Arizona

"The Law is after me," Monroe McPheters says.
"I better pull out of this Guadalupe Canyon way before dark.
 There are no lights on my horse trailer and the Douglas law is waitin'.
 I was ridin' a colt down the alley between F and G Avenue.
 I stopped and went into the B & P Palace to have a drink.
 Well you know, the Law considers a horse a movin' vehicle.
 I didn't realize I'd tied him in a no parkin' zone.
 They gave me two drunk drivin' tickets. They took away my driver's license.
 But next time I come to town I was ready for 'em.
 I rode a colt that was just a little bronky.
 I tied him to that telephone pole by the B & P Bar.
 Went inside and waited for the Law. Well, after a while they found that colt.
 They come into the bar to issue me a ticket.
 I guess I resisted a little so they handcuffed me.
 They threw me into the back of their paddy wagon.
 They asked what I wanted done with that colt.
 I told them they could do any damn thing they wanted,
 Ride him, lead him, or tow him away.
 Well one of them policeman thought he'd ride that colt out of town.
 He only lasted maybe a block or two.
 He was a-layin' on the ground and the colt was runnin' loose.
 The police radioed for other squad cars to come help.
 They had their sirens a-goin' a-tryin'
 To catch that horse runnin' away down the street.
 Well the way to get close to a colt
 Ain't by chasin' him down the road with a siren goin'.
 After awhile they took them handcuffs offa me,
 Let me out of the back of that paddy wagon.
 They said, 'Monroe, you go catch that colt, and you go get on him,
 And you get him and yourself out of this town and don't never come back.'
 That's how I come to settle in Bisbee."

—Voice of MONROE McPHETERS

A Drifting Hippie Girl, Hitchhiking, Living in Bisbee, Arizona

"Well, what are you doing, living there?" Drum asks.
"Well," she says, "It's like the last best part of yourself
Was last seen there, before you lost it,
So you stay there in that place where you lost it,
Still trying to find your last, best part.
And that's how come I'm living in Bisbee."

Religion, Mormons

Haymore Feed Store

Betty Haymore said to her husband, Leonard,
"Cynthia Ann Smith hasn't made any payments
On her overdue bill in the last three months."
Leonard said, "Well, she's a poor old widow woman
Living alone out there in the valley.
I guess I'll have to take care of her."

Goin' to Phoenix to Buy a Stock Trailer
The Jack Mormon and Charles de Gaulle

"I was born into the Mormon Church,
   Born and raised in it," old Dave, the trailermaker, says,
"But anybody who tells me they read
   Holy scripture dug up out of the ground,
   Writ on a goddamn gold plate,
   Lookin' through a flappin' rock, is crazy."
   Within twenty minutes of sayin' that,
   Old Dave was struck down by a heart attack.
"Belief, belief," says Charles de Gaulle,
"Only children and fools believe.
   The Russians believe in things for reasons
   That would make a Frenchman go to sleep.
   Belief is idiocy,
   But nothing great can ever be done without it."

                            —*Voice of* DAVE *the trailermaker*

A Bird in the Hand Is Worth Two in the Bush

Smokey and the Bird Watcher, Cave Creek, Arizona

There's a bird watcher, stealthily stalking up the canyon,
Trying to catch a glimpse of a trogon, a very elusive, migratory bird.
Instead, Smokey Middleton drives up,
Unloads his camper, his wife, his kids, and a dog or two,
Pulls out a lawn chair, and sits down
To enjoy the experience of the great outdoors.
"Mister," says the bird watcher, "could you folks
Please be a little more quiet?
I'm trying to get a closer look at that rare bird over there,
That's singing on the other side of the canyon."
"Feller," says Smokey, "if you'll just hand me
That there shotgun a-leanin' against the tree,
I'll give you a closer look at that bird."

—Voice of SMOKEY MIDDLETON

COURTSHIP BEHAVIOR

From Billy Brown
To the Galaxies

The great galaxy of the Milky Way
Turning in and out about itself
Each word, each thought
So, from that breeding darkness
The light of life is formed
For who we are forever
Is forever being born

• • • • •

TURQUOISE STONES IN THE CREEK BED ...
                THE SOUND OF THE HORSE'S HOOVES IN THE SAND.

A Different Kind of Tune

Prohibition and Country Dances

Well, one time, there was a dance over the hill at Cloverdale.
It was out under the blackjack oak limbs.
It was between the arroyo and the fork in the road.
It was where they'd been a-stealin' old Lee Howard's whiskey.
Every time there was a Cloverdale dance,
They'd let him have a few drinks.
After he was good and liquored up, they'd get his bottle.
Then it was kinda hard for old Lee to remember
Just where he'd hidden it.
But finally, Lee figured out what they was a-doin'.
He poured some of his whiskey into a bottle,
Then he filled the rest of that bottle with croton oil,
You know, that's that damn laxative
That they give to cattle and horses.
After he filled it, he shook it and took that bottle
And he hid it out in the oak brush.
He hid it, but not too good.
Well, one of those boys was pretty proud of hisself.
He'd found Lee's bottle and stole it,
And he was a-dancin' with the prettiest girl there.
They was a-sparkin', just a-whirlin' around,
Across that old Cloverdale dance floor slab.
They was a-do-si-doin' to beat all hell,
Till he began to feel that croton oil start to hit him.
I'll tell you, any bottle of old Lee's that they stole after that,
They sure sniffed around that bottle quite a bit,
And they was damn sure careful about drinkin' it.
I'll tell you that old boy with that croton oil,
He left his pretty girl and he lit out for the far oaks,
And when he ran, he ran a-dancin',
But he was dancin' to a different kind of a tune.

—*Voice of* WALTER RAMSEY

Night Work

Sixty-eight Black Calves

"I think I may change my bulls," Warner says.
"These damn Hereford bulls spend all of their time
A-chasin' them cows in heat,
And then when that cow finally gets ready for 'em,
Those darn bulls are too give out to do anythin' about it.
But that old black bull, who's been a-layin' over there,
Under them mesquites, like he's half-way asleep,
He's been a-watchin'.
He may not know nothin', but he's had his eye on that old cow,
And by golly, when he sees her a-givin' him the sign,
He raises that big old rear end of his off the ground,
Comes over to her kinda slow, by golly, he gives her the business.
In the daytime, the Herefords'll try to hook him off while he's a-breedin'.
They get jealous, just like some men do,
But at night, they can't see that black bastard.
I had a pasture with a hundred and thirty-eight head of cows in it.
I had ten Hereford bulls and one black Angus,
And that Black Angus had a big abcess right behind his tooth.
I got sixty-eight black calves.
Think what he coulda done without a toothache.
I was afraid he might be give out, so I bought two other black bulls.
I only saw him breed one cow once, in the daytime, all Summer.
He's a kind of a rank son of a gun.
I was ridin' a colt, one time a while ago, and he charged.
He hemmed that colt and me up against a side of the corral.
I thought he was goin' to kill that colt.
I pulled out my pistol to shoot him, but he backed off.
I almost killed the best bull I had.
He's like some of these boys in the bars.
He's sure good, but he works mostly at night."

—Voice of WARNER GLENN

Somnambulism
Sleep Deprivation

Louis and Louise Taylor had been makin' all the bars in Douglas.
Allene saw Louise the next day.
Louise's face was all blue and puffed up,
She could just barely see out of one eye.
Allene asked Louise what had happened.
"Well," said Louise, "it was last night,
I come into my room in the Palomar Hotel,
I seen my bed, just a-goin' around and around the room,
I stood there, and I watched that bed go by a few times.
I said to that bed, 'You sucker you, I'll catch you on the next round.'
I just ploughed right into the wall." "Yep," says Allene,
"Sometimes it's hard to find a good place to bed down."

—Voice of ALLENE TAYLOR

Mating Calls

Widows Goin' By

"Now the other day, Mildred Hanigan and I
Were driving up the road to Elfrida to buy hay," says Allene.
"We were passin' by Joe Glenn's place,
We tooted the horn as we went by.
When we'd gotten the hay on the way back,
We stopped to see old Joe. We told him,
'Joe, when we toot that horn to you, that means
There's widows goin' by.'
'Now, I don't have any hay,' Joe Glenn says,
'But any time you girls are lookin' for anything else,
You just stop right here and knock on my door.'"
"Did you hear him, did you hear him?"
Mildred Hanigan says to Allene.
"I heard him, I heard him!" says Allene.
Yep, peet peet, there's widows goin' by.

The moral of this poem is:
Girls and boys, women and men,
As we get older and older
Whoever we were,
Just keeps goin' on and on forever.

—Voices of MILDRED HANIGAN *and* ALLENE TAYLOR

Courtship Behavior

Tellin' Time

"I love you Beeley," the Lady of the Night says.
"Give me a little watch, give me a little lady's watch."
"Goddamn," says Billy Brown,
"I bet I've given every woman in Mexico a watch.
Hell, those people down there
Couldn't wake up in the morning without me.
You ask any woman from Juarez to Mexicali what time it is.
She'll say, *'Ay, déjame ver mi Bilito.'*
'Ah, let me look at my little billy. It is three in the morning.
Ay, Bilito, come with me.
With you, I make love for free.
The fifty dollars, it is for the room.'"

—*Voices of the* THE LADY OF THE NIGHT *and* BILLY BROWN

Boys and Girls

I call up an old girlfriend,
Send a message to her to come out with me tonight.
Instead she sends her husband to the telephone.
She's using me to make him jealous.
He tells me where I can shove it,
And then where I can go ...
For an old girlfriend,
Sometimes a man's worth more dead than alive.

In the burnt brick barroom of the Gadsden Hotel, Billy sits.
His yellow eyes look like still-warm
Puddles of stud piss with the foam blowed off.
Charming wastrel, inviting people,
Offering the hotel's free appetizers
As though they were his own.
"Have these mountain oysters," he says,
"There ain't nothin' fer which more's
Sacrificed in the way of food."

A Lotta Class

Mexico Steer Buyer Billy Brown in Love in the Springtime, on a Street Corner, in Front of the Gadsden Hotel

A pretty girl passes by.
"These Bisbee hippie fillies's got a lotta class," he says,
"It's the only thing they can afford."
He tips his hat,
"Howdy ma'am, lick your leg?
Always tell 'em something they don't think
You're smart enough to invent.
Dazzle 'em with brilliance,
Baffle 'em with bullshit.
Aw, my poor old tally-whacker's a-goin' thump,
Thump, thump like a toad's throat.
My heart feels like it's a-goin' to break.
Promise 'em the rainbow; give 'em the rain.
I can tell this is goin' to be a hard one.
My old wing-ding's feelin' blue as a chicken gizzard."
Chicken gizzards, toad's throats, and rainbows—
Billy Brown, in love, in the Springtime.

—Voice of BILLY BROWN

The Borderline

Keeping Warm in the Old Gadsden Hotel in the Wintertime

One morning, just about that time
You could see the dawnlight seeping into the East,
Billy Brown was coming back to his room in the Gadsden Hotel.
He was coming after a visit he had made to the good ladies of the night,
There, across the line, in the red-light district, in Agua Prieta.
By some miracle, he recognized Mr. Madsen,
The hotel owner, in the Gadsden Hotel lobby.
Billy stopped Mr. Madsen. He poked the finger of his left reining hand
Into the fumes of the Jim Beam whiskey air floating around him.
"Mr. Madsen, sir," he said,
"Either I want that steam heat in my room fixed right away,
Or I want you to send up three blankets,
Along with two Mexican ladies of the night immediately."
Old Billy went prancing off up the marble stone steps and was gone.
The steam heat still clicks in the radiator pipes,
Just about dawnlight in the mornings.

—Voice of BILL BRYAN

Love

I. Gettin' Hitched

"Horses are a lot like women," says Trog Smith,
"There are ones that you think a lot of,
  And ones that you don't think nothin' of.
  Ones that you can get the day's work done on,
  Or maybe, the next time you try,
  It's a-gonna be a little bit better.
  Kind of reminds me of my wife.
  I was ridin' a bronky mare one time,
  You could do about anything you wanted on her,
  As long as it was serious business.
  But if you went to screwin' around,
  That damn bitch would buck you off every time.
  But you know, you fall in love
  With one of these pretty girls,
  You court 'em and then live with 'em.
  For about ten years, you think you've got a friend."

— Voice of TROG SMITH

II. Marriage and a Windmiller

  Like old Carl, the windmiller,
  Said when his truck broke down,
  And he'd walked nine miles through the desert
  In the dark to the Cross Rail Ranch,
  Where Bill Bryan and me were sitting in the twilight,
  After he made a call to his wife to get help,
"By God, yuh live with a woman twenty-five years,
  She don't know who you are on a telephone?
  We gotta get some things straightend out.
  Well, I identified myself, an' all ...
  'Oh,' she says, 'It's you.'"

III. Halter Horses and Women

Now some women are halter women
And some women are usin' women.
Now if they got their legs set a little bit under 'em
And got a pretty good rear end on 'em,
They can sure wheel and turn and hold your rope good,
But they may not halter.
Now to halter, you got to have one who's got a good eye,
A good head, who travels straight.
And you got to notice their front end.
They got to V up real good in front,
If they don't V up, they're too flat and they won't handle.
A horse, like a woman, has got to have balance.
Their rear end has got to get down in the dirt
And work just right with their front end,
But they got to have forward motion at the same time.

—Voice of TROG SMITH

IV. Splittin' the Blanket

You got a mare and she's a good mare,
You can't afford to be mean to her.
She'll kick your damn head off.
I once had a bay mare who was kind of bronky,
Always a-prancin' around and a-fidgetin'.
You could catch her all right, but she always made you wonder
If she was a-gonna reach up
With one of them prancin' hooves, and strike you in the head,
Straighten you out.
Kind of reminds me of my wife.
I fell in love with a gal one night 'cause I was drinkin',
She was a dirty good son of a buck, but a hard keeper.
If you don't give her all the money you got,
She ain't a-gonna work for you no way.

I just got out of the hospital.
I'd been a-ridin' a young mare for the last two or three weeks.
She didn't have in mind what I had in mind.
So I whopped her over the head,
She come over backwards.
The saddle horn hit my belt buckle,
And buried itself plumb in the middle of my stomach.
Horses are a lot like a woman,
You knock 'em around a little,
They're either afraid of you,
Or you're afraid of them.
They'll take you to court.
Kinda reminds me of that woman
Who used to be my wife.

—Voice of TROG SMITH

CIVILIZATION

Cowboys and Chainsaws

"Hello, Bud. What happened to you?"
  His hands all swathed up in bandages,
"Aw, the chain saw got me," he says.
"Was it idlin'?" I ask him.
"No, it was churnin' along pretty good," he says,
"If it hadda worked better,
  It woulda cut my hand off."
"Well, it's a good thing it didn't work too well," says Drum.
"It won't work at all now," says Bud,
"I threw it as far as I could."

—*Voice of* BUD ROBBINS

• • • • •

TURQUOISE STONES IN THE CREEK BED ...
            THE SOUND OF THE HORSE'S HOOVES IN THE SAND.

Capitalism

The Smugglers

I.

    "In prohibition time," says Walter,
    "Things was pretty lively in this border country.
      Harry Wilson was the biggest bootlegger in these parts.
      He was a pretty smart feller.
      I reckon he knew every canyon and rat bin in two counties.
      One time the Law was a-trompin' on his tail.
      He come to a gate in the fence
      That runs across that road near Baker Canyon.
      Him and his driver come a-screechin'
      To a halt in front of that gate.
      They opened it and went on through.
      Then they got out a big piece of trace chain
      And a padlock and locked that chain around the gate.
      Well they got away from the Law that time
    'Cause it wasn't very good policy
    To tear somebody's fence down,
    Specially if you was the Law."

II.

    "Another time the Law, who was O. E. Patterson,
      Caught 'em bringin' in a load of mescal,
      When they got a flat tire by Rodeo.
      Well, they fixed that tire
      And Harry Wilson told his driver
      To get in the car and drive it up a little.
      Old Harry tightened a lug nut.
      That driver of his,
      He'd creep that dang car up a little bit further,
      And old Harry Wilson'd tighten another lug nut.
      Then they'd creep it up again a little bit further.
      They kept that up,
      Till they got all of the nuts tight,

And the car was a little ways off from O. E. Patterson.
Then Harry Wilson rared up
And throwed his arms around Patterson
And yelled to his driver to take off.
Patterson struggled with him for a while.
They was both big men.
Old Harry Wilson, he just stayed with him
Until that car and that load was off down the road.
'I got a good mind to kill you,'
O. E. Patterson said to Harry Wilson.
'You got a better mind than that,' Harry Wilson said.
Patterson took Wilson to see the judge.
'I caught him again, Judge,' he said.
But that judge asked, 'Where's the evidence?'
The driver'd already brought the mescal
Into town and sold it.
That judge said to Patterson, 'Turn him loose,'
And that old Harry Wilson got away again."

III.
    "Another time, O. E. Patterson caught Harry
    And was a-takin' him into town.
    Both was in their cars and a-rollin' along pretty good
    Till Harry Wilson pulled over to the side of the road.
    When O. E. Patterson come up to see what's wrong,
    Wilson's driver tells him they'd run out of gas.
    The driver asked if they could borrow
    Enough gas from Patterson to get into Douglas.
    They looked around for a can to put the gas in.
    The driver crawled around under O. E. Patterson's car.
    They filled that little can about four or five times,
    To where they figured Patterson was a-foolin' around
    And not payin' too much attention.
    Then, that driver put the plug back into that gas tank,
    But he only give it about a quarter turn.
    They got back into their cars and headed towards Douglas.
    After a while old O. E. Patterson began to slowly fall behind.

When Wilson and his driver seen that,
They really floor-boarded that gas pedal.
Then while Patterson was a-waitin'
Out there on that highway, fit to be tied, a-tryin'
To get somebody to stop and to give him some gas,
Old Harry Wilson sold his load of mescal
And got plumb away again.
That old Harry Wilson, he wasn't born under no rock."

IV.
   "Did they ever get you, Walter?" Drum asks.
   "I never did have the Law
    Get that close to me," says Walter.
  "I went through that real rough country,
    Just East of the Puerta Colorada, with a pack mule,
    And if the Law was that close, I didn't know it.
    A fair-size mule can trot along pretty good
    With twenty gallons of mescal on a pack frame,
    Two ten-gallon kegs, that is, if they're full,
    And you damn sure want 'em full.
    I used to bring mescal from the Devil's Canyon,
    Down in Mexico for Old Man Bill McDonald.
    It was pretty good for a while,
    Men live by what people believe in or don't believe in,
    But when the country went wet,
    It put everybody out of business.
    It damn sure did."
  "I'll try to put this in a poem," says Drum.
  "Well, it would be a hell of a poem, I'll bet,"
   Old Walter says.
   And it dang sure is.

—Voice of WALTER RAMSEY

The Law

The Law and Old-Time Cowboys

Driving slowly, peacefully into town,
On a beautiful Spring day, February 17, 1981,
There's old Walter Ramsey on the curve
By the windmill, just East of town.
"The Law is after you," he says,
"Better oil up your six-shooter.
Somethin' about the haulin' papers
For them damn mares you finally got rid of.
Your wife says they're goin' to put you in jail.
Goddamn, it's gettin' so a man can't hardly do nothin' no more,
Without a-turnin' around and seein' the damn Law
A-trompin' too close on his tail.
A man can't hardly run one of these ranches.
He's got to spend half his time fillin' out papers
He's lost somewheres.
Hell, it's gettin' too damn complicated nowadays,
For a man to be a cowboy or a rancher.
Turn around and come with me to Mexico.
We'll find us one of them old Indian caves.
We'll ride a ways down South of the border.
We'll tell the Law to go to hell."

—Voice of WALTER RAMSEY

Two Cattle Contracts

Same family, seventy-three years apart, shown to Drum by a Mormon bishop, Leonard Haymore, at Haymore Feed Store

I.

Deben por el siguiente ganado
Con las marcas al margen se estampan
They owe for the following cattle
Whose brands are stamped on the margin ...

To be paid on delivery:
100 novíos de un año $8.00 c/u,
100 one-year-old steers $8.00 a head
60 steers, two years old, $12.00 a head
40 three-year-old steers $18.00 a head

3% tax *al estado*, to the state	$67.20
1.5% *sibre*/federal	$16.80
Timbres, stamps	$13.44
Total	$2,337.44

Colonia Oaxaca 1º de mayo, the first of May, 1906
Signed Millard Haymore
Rafael Lamadrid, Cattle Inspector, Bavispe, Mexico

II.
  "Leonard and Lovell Haymore will sell to Everett Campbell
  Fifty head of steer calves ninety-five cents per pound.
  Cattle are Brangus type, branded on left hip
  And located at Castle Dome Ranch, Silver Creek, Arizona.
  Cattle are to be delivered to the Bar M Ranch
  And weighed off of trucks with no shrink."
  The deal sealed with a handshake and a look in the eye,
  Douglas, Arizona, Springtime of 1979.

  Drum shakes his head, "1906—steers eight dollars a head.
  1979—steers ninety-five cents a pound,
  Three hundred eighty dollars a head.
  In 1906, Leonard's dad drove a buggy,
  Today his brother drives a Lincoln."

The Fire

Justice and Landmark Cases

Well, Judge Oscar Frank was in a house of the good ladies
One night in Agua Prieta, when a fire broke out.
The judge didn't happen to have any pants on just at that moment.
To save his life, he went streaking out to his car, naked,
Grabbed the handle of the door,
Yanked on the door-handle, to escape,
And realized that he had left his car keys
In his pants pocket, back in the burning house of the good ladies.
Naked justice—a man's worst dream.
The judge borrowed a towel from someone,
Wrapped it around his middle,
Went to a telephone to call his wife to come save him.
As Old Man Ben Williams said,
"She must have been a very understanding woman.
Either that, or she didn't understand anything at all."
The judge was known for his delicate handling of the law,
Especially of women in divorce cases.
He had a soft, blue, leather sofa in his consulting office
And the majority of the women who came in his office
Usually won their trial.
His ruling is still studied in a landmark case
For the "rat in the bean can,"
In the field of products liability, Haggerty versus Simms.
But really, he was a mean son-of-a-bitch,
Though he was always nice to women.
He fell down the steps one day and died.
The strange thing was,
That it was one of the few times he was not drinking.
Old Cramm, who is still practicing law in Bisbee today,
Went to the cemetery to piss on his grave.
That was The Law of Cochise County,
In the mid part of the twentieth century.

Law on the Borderline

One Honest Client

"Look, people don't come to a lawyer for justice," says Lou Boroni.
"They come because they are getting hassled or screwed,
 Or they want to hassle or to screw someone else.
 In the twenty-three years I have practiced law,
 There has only been one honest client who came to me.
 She was a little old Mexican woman.
 '*Abogado*, lawyer,' she said, 'I have come to you
 Because I have a problem. Some years ago
 I borrowed eight hundred dollars from a man.
 Now he wants me to pay it back.
 He says he will sue me if I don't pay him.
 Will you help me fight him?'
 'Well,' I said, 'court is very expensive.
 It sounds as though the simplest and most honest thing
 Would be for you to simply pay the man
 The eight hundred dollars you owe him.'
 '*Abogado*, lawyer,' she said, 'I certainly didn't have to come
 All the way to your office to hear advice like that.'"

• • • • •

TURQUOISE STONES IN THE CREEK BED ...
        THE SOUND OF THE HORSE'S HOOVES IN THE SAND.

THE TEACHINGS OF
BRONC BUSTER BILLY BROWN

Crop Failure

The Man Called Billy Brown

The wildest, horse-ridin'est, whiskey-drinkin'est,
Woman-chasin'est cowboy
Who's rode all of this desert country
From Texas along the Rio Grande a-sowin' his wild oats
And a-prayin' for crop failure.
"I'm a lover and a fighter and a wild horse rider
And I'm a pretty fair windmill man too," old Billy would say.
"Do you savvy? Are you listenin'?"

Tall, skinny Texan in black high-heeled boots,
A dancer who moves on his toes into the stirrups.
Legend of horse breaking gone to Mexico to escape the Law.
Near sixty years old, hair beginning to grey;
Four-inch-brim sombrero pulled way down
Over his eyes to keep the desert sun from burning.
His wages go to fine gear, rawhide, horsehair hackamores,
Bits, a pair of silver spurs with the letters "BILLY,"
A tooled saddle, soft batwing chaps.
A pretty tough hombre, some people say;
If another man doesn't return his Southern-drawled politeness.

The Nature of a Cowboy

I. The Hiring of Billy Brown

"There just ain't many old-time cowpunchers around,
Who know as much about horses as he does.
You sure oughta get him to ride them colts,
And you'd learn a lot from him too," Bud says.
"Well," says Drum, "we've got five colts he could ride.
They're all started but one.
I don't think they'd buck or hurt him,
But my wife'd sure throw a terrible fit
If I brought another drinker to the ranch.
We've already got Roberto and Walter and Juan.
And Carlos and Berto would go along with 'em,
And old Billy would sure set 'em off,
If they got the chance."
"Well, would your wife get over it?" says Bud.
"I guess she'd cool off, Bud, in maybe three or four weeks."
Bud throws his saddle onto his horse, laughs, and rides away.
"Well, the quicker you do it, the quicker she'll get over it."

—Voice of BUD ROBBINS

On the Square of the Red-Light Houses
in Agua Prieta

*Billy Brown worked for Chapo Varela at the Rancho Nuevo in the Cajón Bonito. Chapo
paid Billy Brown to ride colts, but he paid him with mares instead of money.*

II. Hunting for Billy Brown

The lights blinking red and orange and blue and green,
Old lime paint flaking off the adobe walls,
The horns, the music of the mariachis playing,
Soft light, yellow and warm inside.
"I'm a lover and a fighter and a wild horse rider
And just a pretty fair windmill man. Do you savvy, are you listenin'?
Goddamn, I think I been off with a darn *puto*.
I took her back to one of them rooms.
I took her clothes off and she didn't have no chichis!"
"Dame un piece, price," one says.
"Se levanta pura madre," says another.
A coyote calling off in the desert country to the South,
Yip yip yip ooooooooooooourh.
"My goddamn false teeth are loose," Billy says.
"I don't know whether I could bite one of 'em on the tittie or not,
But I'm a-gonna try."
He goes and gets another one, ·
Comes back after a while.
"She was old enough not to lie to me.
You know the young ones, they'll all lie.
We talked about horses.
I don't know how much a horse does think,
But they're like a woman. They understand quite a bit,
But in a hundred years from now—
Why, I've seen people a-killin' themselves,
Runnin' around tryin' to get things done—
In a hundred years from now, it won't make any difference,
Rich or poor, so you better smell the goddamn flowers.
Smell 'em while you ride on by.

You know," says Billy Brown, "I think I'll get me a pack outfit,
A Springerville tree, take these old mares,
If I can't legally get 'em across the borderline,
And ride on South to Sahuaripa.
That's where they got them big chi-chis."

• • • • •

A pretty green-eyed girl comes to sit
On the lip of the bar stool beside him.
"Green, green, how I like green," says Billy Brown.
"You know, I never could figure out which I liked best,
Green eyes or green grass.
I think I used to like green eyes best,
But now, I think I like green grass."

—*Voice of* BRONC BUSTER BILLY BROWN

The Study of Ancient Literature

III. By the Old Cantina Oak Wood Bar
Billy Brown Considers the Bible
Genesis, Chapter 19, Verse 26:
Lot Fleeing from the Wrath of the Lord

"You know, that Bible's not a bad book," Billy Brown says.
"It's a little slow in parts, but they fight,
They drink the booze, they sleep with other men's wives.
Why, it's got almost everything in it.
One time, I bet a feller a case of Jim Beam whiskey
The Bible even told about a man a-sleepin' with one of his daughters.
That was the story about that old feller Lot who was on the dodge,
And runnin' from the Law, and him and his daughters slipped off.
They went to live in a cave for a while.
Well, after they'd been there in that cave for about three years,
These young fillies was a-comin' along in their teens,
And they was a-feelin' kinda hot and twisty like.
Do you savvy, are you listenin'?
Now their old daddy, he liked to drink the booze.
Well, one night these girls ups and gets their old daddy drunk,
And when they had him pretty good and lickered up,
After he'd gone to bed, one of these fillies,
Feelin' kinda hot and twisty like,
Why, she climbs into the bed with him.
Well, her old daddy gives her the business, he does.
And because he had those drinks a couple of thousand years ago,
I won that case of Jim Beam whiskey!
Do you savvy, are you listenin'?"

—Voice of BRONC BUSTER BILLY BROWN

A Bottle of Jim Beam Whiskey

IV. Bringing Billy Brown to the Ranch to Ride Colts

Slip him up to the camp by the spring, quick,
So none of the other cowboys will see him,
Catch that wild look, quit their work,
And run off on a rampage to town.
"Billy, I can't take you out there," I tell him.
"Not if you've got any more
Bottles of Jim Beam whiskey.
It's too much to do to Diana.
We've done enough to her already.
You don't have any more, do you?"
"No! No!" Billy says.
But when he gets up to the spring somewhere,
He finds one down in the curls of his bedroll.
Goddamn, that's three more days of wild drunkenness
I'll have to go through.
But when he gets good and drunk, I do get the secret
From him, about where he's hid some more.
I may have had to unscrew those back hinges
Off his locked truck, but I got that damn bottle.
"Billy do you have any more whiskey?"
I ask him the next day.
"NO, NO," he says.
"Can I have any I find then, Billy?"
"Well, I guess so," he says.
Goddamn, I got Billy Brown that time.
Got his bottle of Jim Beam whiskey.
Got it now and it's hidden away, too.

—*Voice of* BRONC BUSTER BILLY BROWN

By the Sandy Picket Corral

V. To Hackamore the Colt

"¿Dónde está el Beeley? Yo creo que estudia su brujería.
Where is Billy? I'll bet he's studyin' his witchcraft." Roberto laughs.
Roberto and Drum are waiting for him by the sandy picket corral.
Moved him last week from his camp by the spring.
"Where is old Billy?"
"Hell, he's fallen asleep again in the bunkhouse.
We've got our ropes ready.
We need him to come help us,
To give us some of his magic, to slip a hackamore easy
Onto this jumping, kicking, little Bayleaf colt."
Two weeks later, finally, he comes walking, bowlegged, down
By the sandy picket corral to hackamore the colt.
Listen to the sound of the rope.
His thrown rope swishes through the air,
Ropes him quick with a hoolihan loop.
Hollers to us to come help pull.
"Pull, pull hard on the rope!
Watch that colt. He's rarin'!
Don't let him go over backward.
If he hits on his top knot, it'll kill him.
Get a hitch over your hip on that rope.
Get his ear! Get his tail!
Get his ear! Lift his tail!
There, we got him stopped."

‐Voices of BRONC BUSTER BILLY BROWN *and* ROBERTO ESPINOSA

A Pat on the Ass

VI. In These Flying Seconds

The stillness goin' by too fast.
"Quick, before he quits restin' and starts fightin' again,
Tie up that colt's back foot. Hobble him in front,
Hobble him behind,
Sideline him!
Sack him out with a light saddle blanket,
While he stands there, quiverin' with his eyes all wide."
Billy ropes him time and again,
Holding him close by the hackamore lead,
Takes off the foot ropes, drops a loop over his rump,
Twitches it to scare him, to teach him to lead.
In less than an hour from when he first felt the rope
Settle around the soft mane hair on his neck,
The colt's got a saddle on, following Billy around the corral.
"Billy, that sure was a pretty job," says Drum.
"Well you know," Billy says, breathing a little hard,
"Just about the time you get old enough
To know what you're doin',
You're so old and sored up,
You can't do it anymore.
Instead of takin' a pretty girl off to bed her down somewhere,
You just want to sit here,
And drink a cold beer or give her a pat on her ass.
Where is she?
I'm not that old yet.
Come on. Let's get a drink of water.
We'll ride the rest of these colts before the sun goes down.
We'll ride 'em all down the canyon a ways."

—Voice of BRONC BUSTER BILLY BROWN

· · · · ·
To Be Tied Hard and Fast

When Billy Brown was dying in the veterans' hospital,
In Tucson, Arizona, he kept trying to escape,
Like the mule Mike, back to his *querencia*,
the big, wild, open country of the Sierra Madre.

The nurses had put handcuffs on him.
They were made of plastic,
but in his weakened condition,
They might as well have been made of steel.
He said, "Drum, cut me loose ... cut me loose."
This poem is called "Cutting Loose in the Springtime."

Cutting Loose in the Springtime

I.

Billy Brown, being an old Texas cowboy,
Was a hard and fast tie man.
That means he tied his rope solid,
Or fast, to the saddle horn, as against dallying.
Dallying means to take turns of the rope around the saddle horn,
To hold an animal you've got roped,
So if something happens and you start to get into a wreck,
You can let your rope slide around the saddle horn,
Or take those dallies off the horn.
Billy only dallied roping little calves in a corral,
'Cause, he said, you had to learn it when you were young,
Or you couldn't do it well enough to keep from losing
A finger, or a hand, or a thumb.
Billy carried a knife strapped to his chaps right above his thigh bone,
So if he had a cow brute, or some critter roped,
And he was tied hard and fast,
And was maybe riding a spinning, pitching colt,
With the coils of that rope winding around him,
He could pull his knife free, and start cutting loose.

II.

Sometimes, Spring comes whirling up these desert canyons
From the South so strong, I'd cut loose and go a-prancing...
With one of these light seeds that flies up towards the canyon rim.
Sometimes, those sweet scents of the Springtime
Come whirling up these draws from Mexico so strong,
When the blood-weed starts greening up,
And the mourning doves start calling long,
Long into the beginning of the morning

III.

When the Spring winds come blowing down the ridge lines,
And you feel them blowing along the creased lines of your skin,
Who would tell Springtime to be still,
Or to go away from the rims of these dry canyons and hills,
Till all the honey and all the humming bees,
And those light blue eyes are gone?
Who would tell the Springtime to be still?

BOOK THREE

· · · · ·

Changes

· · · · ·

• • • • •

TURQUOISE STONES IN THE CREEK BED ...

THE SOUND OF THE HORSE'S HOOVES IN THE SAND.

PREAMBLE

The Canyon

Cloud shadows and sunlight crossing the rocks,
Spanish dagger blooms on the ridgelines and mountaintops.
You and I and all of those years
In the dawnlight, who can remember now?

Across the Stretch of These Desert Rangelands

The people will come to be with the light mesquite leaves,
Turning here in the Springtime they will come,
To be with the mesas, the valleys of yellow flowers,
Slashing flames of gold and red and green,
The stretch of blue mountain ranges ringing the breaks.
They will come to know
The voices of the desert, its peoples.
The horizons rising and falling again and again
Into those fabled blue cradled lands.
Out of the distances, valley upon fading valley,
Blue breaking range upon range,
Ringing forever, rising forever, again and again.
Each lion, each bear, each antelope, each jaguar,
Crossing the arroyo rock cuts of this land.
The still tilting wings of the vulture, the black hawk, the eagle
Crossing above the cliffs of the Cajón Bonito.
With that desert stillness ringing in their ears they will come
To know those shaded shapes of this fading old Earth.
Hearts mixing, stretching outward
In these healing flames of the desert rangelands.

Racing the Sun

Hey, let's see if we can beat the morning light
To the edge of the cliff rocks and back,
Before the light hits the far North peaks.
Come on, are you ready?
Hurry up, let's go.

The Trail

By a cut bank where there are seep willows,
Where the leaves of a *sacahuista* grow in from the South,
That's where the first trace of this trail begins,
In the sunlight and rains, in the clouds and the Winter snows,
In the blowing leaves, old hoofprints on the trail,
Coming from somewhere up the canyon ...
Come on, let's follow it, then we'll know where it goes.

Getting Old

Leaf Shadows

Drum is riding down the canyon.
He comes to where Walter has his camp
Beside the spring by the sycamore tree.
"Come on," says Walter,
"Light down off your horse
To sit a spell with me.
We'll sit here and tell some tales.
We'll follow those high leaf shadows,
Falling down to the ground around us.
Leaf shadows and tales,
You and I and this sycamore tree."

THE BORDERLINE

If you listen closely,
There are the other whispersoft voices
To be heard along this Borderline.
Not strong, not loud, not imposing,
But they are there.

TURQUOISE STONES IN THE CREEK BED ...
       THE SOUND OF THE HORSE'S HOOVES IN THE SAND.

Migrant Labor

The Texas Borderline

Es una cosa muy triste, cruzando la frontera.
It is a very sad thing, crossing the Borderline.
Nos niegan cruzar. They stop us from crossing.
Uno tiene que venir. One has to come.
One has to cross over with hunger, with thirst, crying.

—*Voice of* YOLANDA FLORES

Mexican Men

They come whistling,
With nothing more than the shirt on their backs,
Walking across the Borderline.
They have no money.
They speak no English.
They leave hungry families behind them.
When they are cold,
They light a *sacahuista* fire.
When they are hot and thirsty,
They sit in the shade.
They hope to come to water soon.
Some never do.

Dreams

Song of the Mexican's Wife

De tantas partes que hemos conocido,
Why, in all of the places that we have known,
Hasta americanos y japoneses y de todas razas,
Including Americans and Japanese and all the races,
Y en todos los ranchos donde hemos trabajado,
And all of the ranches that we have worked on,
¿Por qué no estamos ricos?
How can it be that we have not become rich?
I am thinking, still,
That someday, we will be rich.

According to Whose Law

Selling Out

Wednesday
A man from the Livestock Sanitary Board
Came to Len and Sadie Hinman's ranch.
He picked up an unbranded colt that had crossed through
The boundary fence from Mexico.
According to the laws of the United States,
He took that colt to be sold at the Hanlon livestock sale.

Thursday morning, auction day
"If anybody buys that colt," says Sadie Hinman,
"They're sure gonna have to pay a lot to get him."
Sadie and Len went to the auction, bought that colt,
They hauled him back to their ranch on the border.

Friday
"Old Len's gonna lose a horse," Waylon says.

Saturday
Two shod horses stolen from Len Hinman's canyon pasture,
Tracks headed off towards Mexico.

Sunday
"Old Len may not know it," says Waylon,
"But there's many a rancher that's had to sell out
Here along this Borderline.
Now, what old Len done may a been right
Accordin' to the law, but it was the wrong thing to do,
If you're a-livin' here along this Border.
Anytime a horse or a cow brute comes across that line fence,
The best thing to do is take it down to the Blue Gate crossing.
You better put it on back across the line.
Now when the state seizes an animal that's come from Mexico,
And takes that animal on up to the Hanlon auction,

You better not buy that animal, that is, if you're livin' here along this Border.
Probably the owner of that colt come took Len's horses.
That or they were layin' a trap for him to see what he'd do
When they pushed that colt across.

Monday
"We tracked 'em down the canyon," Len says,
"Into that horse trap by the Blue Gate.
They cut the line fence in a draw.
They went on South down the country.
They rode out on a ridge and through some mares and colts.
They was hidin' their tracks.
We lost a little time there, but the mares were barefooted.
Our stolen horses were shod.
We followed the shod hooves.
The horses we were ridin' was just a-puffin' and a-blowin'.
We could see by the tracks that they was just ahead of us,
But we couldn't seem to catch up with 'em.
Here's what the track of that one feller looked like."
(Len draws a boot print in the sand.)
"He wore *huarache* sandals.
The other feller wore a small cowboy boot,
With one of them underslung heels
A little bit bigger than a penny.
If you see a feller makin' tracks like that, let me know," says Len.
"Maybe it's a good thing you didn't
Come up with those fellers, Len," Waylon says.
"You're damn right, it's a good thing for them," Len says.
"'Cause if we had, the coyotes'd be eatin' 'em."
"You know," says Waylon, "When I see a feller I really don't like,
Chances are I'm just like him."

By the boundary line of old Mexico ...
Bury 'em deep and leave no witnesses ...

    We'll charge it to the wind
    And let the dust settle it.

                          —Voices of WAYLON *and* LEN HINMAN

Prohibition

A Six-Shooter and a .30-.30 Rifle

Old Ed Leahy used to be a-spottin' for us around here.
He used to get up on a high point
With his field glasses and look for us,
But we all crossed the fence at some place
Where we figured he damn sure wouldn't be.
One time Ed Leahy seen old Simón Napoery,
A Mexican who was a-workin' for Ralph McDonald
Down by the Puerta Blanca.
Old Simón broke to run when he seen Ed,
And was a-tryin' to get across to that flat by the line fence.
Well, when Ed Leahy seen old Simone a-runnin',
He just thought it would be funny to take his six-shooter
And shoot near him a few times
To see how fast old Simón could run.
Well, old Simón run all right, he run to where
He had a .30-.30 rifle hid behind a ledge of rock,
And that time it was old Ed's turn to run, 'cause old Ed's six-shooter
Was damn sure no match for that .30-.30 rifle.
Old Ed Leahy said to Ralph McDonald,
"You know that feller you got a-workin' for you is crazy,
He's gonna kill somebody one of these days."
Said Ralph McDonald to old Ed, "I reckon he is, Ed,
He's just about as crazy as you."

—Voice of RALPH McDONALD

Pancho Villa

A Favor

"I wish you'd met old Lem Spilsbury," Smokey Middleton says.
"Him and Pancho Villa was pretty good friends,
   Even though they were on different sides of the Borderline.
   Pancho told Lem, if ever he needed a favor to let him know.
   Well, during the revolution, when Pancho Villa was a-burnin'
   And raidin' on this side of the Borderline, a friend of Lem's
   Asked Lem to go into Mexico and bring back a woman
   Because she was going to have a baby.
   Lem got into his wagon and drove into the town
   Where Pancho Villa was with his army of *vaqueros*.
   They had black moustaches,
   They was swarthy, they had muscles,
   They had pot bellies, they was his children
   And the children of his children.
   'Get down!' said Pancho Villa.
   Lem stepped down out of that wagon,
   Walked over to where Pancho Villa was standing,
   Put his arm on Pancho's shoulder and he said,
   'You remember that favor? This is it.'
   'Get up!' said Pancho Villa.
   Lem stepped up into his wagon, and brought that woman back."

                              —*Voice of* SMOKEY MIDDLETON

Hope

Una vez, a mí me tocó ...
Once, it touched me,
That a woman told me her story.

A Fruit Picker

We went to town.
My husband, he went off and got drunk.
I got a ride back to the orchard with a friend.
When I came close to our camp,
I heard a little rustling in the brush.
It was two of the fruit pickers,
They, who had come back to camp to rape me.
I had seen them partly naked, by a little pool.
It was when they were bathing.
One of them, called Lupe, was a Yaqui Indian,
He started raping me.
At first, it was a little bad,
But I told him he could do what he wanted.
He left the orchard the next day,
But when I went back to the pool by the creek,
I found where he had left me a little piece of candy.
Well, I hope it was for me.

—Voice of ELIZABET VALENZUELA

A Window in the Breeze

Daughter to the lawyer of the Queen of Holland,
Seven years of living in a shack
Beside the Vallecitos Creek, waters flowing past.
All she has left is the way she throws her head
When she moves about the kitchen
To knead and bake the brown bread.
All she has left is the way she throws her pretty head
When the light strands of her long dark hair
Sway through the years from her face to her shoulder.
Two coyotes howling across the lone hills.
Strands of hair, a window in the breeze.

Once a Young Girl

The moment when the bloom of the flower
Is swaying in the wind, sunlight and the drifting clouds
Before the birds and the flies and the sucking ants
Come to drain that flower dry.

Keeping Warm in the Rangeland

A Coat

Alvin Taylor and some *vaqueros*
Was a-cuttin' cattle one day, till all of a sudden,
Alvin looked up from the cow he was cuttin'.
He saw that the cattle they'd already cut were back,
A-mixin' together with the rest of the herd.
Then he saw those Mexican *vaqueros*.
They was a-standin' around a little fire kinda shakin'.
Of course he knew, but he went over.
He asked one of those *vaqueros*
Why in the hell they'd let all the cuts get back into the main herd.
Finally, one of 'em spoke up. Said they'd got cold.
"Jesus Cristo," said Alvin,
"If you'd take that money you earn and go buy a coat
When you get into town, instead of taking it right over
To those ladies of the night,
In the red-light houses in Agua Prieta,
You'd have somethin' that would keep you warm."
They shifted their weight on their feet and smiled.
They remembered other ways to keep warm,
Worth more than the coat on a man's back.

—Voice of ALLENE TAYLOR

By the Fire

If you stand close to the campfire to keep warm
And the heat of the fire goes
Into the fluid in your knees
Then, when you leave the fire,
Your knees will get stiff
And you will have *reumas,*
So don't stand too near the fire in the dawnlight.

—Voice of ROBERTO ESPINOSA

The Poor

A Fire

In a place where there's no wind,
Where the sunlight hits by a dirt bank,
Or a cliff, maybe on a street corner,
You'll find *el sobre de todos los pobres,*
The overcoat of the poor.
There in the warmth of the sunlight.

"Well I've seen a lotta that,"
Walter Ramsey says.
"Some poor *vaquero,*
Just standin' there, a-shiverin' by a fire,
A-waitin' for that warm sunlight to come,
And I've done it too."

—Voice of WALTER RAMSEY

A Welcome Touch

Sunlight

Or some *vaquero,* too poor to buy gloves,
Trying to keep his reining hand warm on the roundup drive.
He puts first one cold hand into his pocket
For a while and then the other,
While he keeps his position in the roundup drive.
Then that first sunlight that strikes
The chilled back of his hand
Is a welcome touch of the Earth's old light.

• • • • •

All I had when I met you
Was a saddle and a bedroll,
And it's all that you have left of me,
Now that I am gone.

To Mexicans and Cold

The Drifting Cowboy

"¿Qué palabras uso para pedir ésta comida?
What words do you use to ask for this food?"
The drifting cowboy says.
Who says the men on this whirling old Earth
Were ever anything but lost?
Sunlight and the leaves passing through these canyons ...
Light dust drifting in the dust
Blowing away in the ruts of the road.
If you don't know you're alone, you're alone.
But for a man, there's never been any woman,
But this whirling old Earth,
Singing to him in the wind that goes calling,
Whirling on past.
"¿Para dónde vas? Where are you headed?" Drum asks him.
"Quién sabe ... Who knows ... to the North," he says,
"Looking for work."
And goes whistling away on down the dirt road.
Dust, and the wind singing behind him ...

—Voice of an unknown cowboy

Coming Out of the Mountains towards Home

Riding through the darkness on a three-year-old bronc
With the chill night wind blowing in February.
Shapes of cedar limbs quivering with shadows and wind,
The bronc trembling light under the soft saddle blankets,
Ready to start bucking if a rabbit runs out from a bush.
Cedar limbs, cliffs and canyon rocks,
Icy stinging Winter wind. With hands numb,
How to keep both hands on the reins
To be ready to spin him when he starts bucking,
I'll hope for the best and keep changing.
One warm hand under my chaps
One cold hand on the reins.
We'll go towards home now, you and me, little colt,
Passing through the rocks and the darkness
The cliffs and ghost shapes of the sycamore trees.
We'll hope we make it home.

All That Ever Is

Rubén

A dirt floor and one kerosene lamp in his home
When Drum worked roundups with him.
Every mornin' as the roundup crew took off at daybreak,
Rubén's horse would be a little humpy with the cold.
He would spur his horse with one *mocho* spur,
The rowel gone, to show off his riding on a bucking horse.
Roped every cow and calf he could.
Best dally hand among the young cowboys,
A good tracker too … so many years
Of lookin' at cows and dust and sand.
He stands beside me at the Guadalupe Ranch twelve years later.
We are watching the bulldozer push sand out of the arroyo.
He is a grown man.
"You can change the Earth with one of those," Drum says,
While the dozer blade is changing the arroyo.
He looks at me with those soft brown Mexican eyes,
Shakes his head and smiles. "No," he says,
"No, you can change the earth a little,
But the earth, the earth stays."

THE TRADERS

Horse Trading

My old Daddy used to say,
"You walk around a horse once.
You look in his mouth.
You're ready to trade.
It's about the same with a man or a woman.
You walk around one of them once.
You see what's in their eyes.
You're ready to trade."

—Voice of ROY THORN

· · · · ·

TURQUOISE STONES IN THE CREEK BED ...
        THE SOUND OF THE HORSE'S HOOVES IN THE SAND.

Economics

Cow Trading by the Rio Grande

Phil Statler had a bunch of cows sold to Ted Rob,
But some of the cows got the jimmies from eatin' poison weed.
They was a-tremblin' and a-shakin' and about to die.
"I'll buy every son of a bitch that walks off the trucks alive," Ted Rob said.
Well about forty of 'em walked off the trucks, and lay down and died.
Old Ted got mad and didn't want to pay.
"I thought you'd take every son of a bitch
That walked off the trucks alive," Phil Statler said.
"They may have walked off," Ted Rob said,
"But they was dead sons of bitches while they was a-walkin'."

—Voices of TED ROB *and* PHIL STADTLER

A Good Horse

Blood in the Eye

Terais was a horse trader.
He had some good horses and one very bad one,
But he made more money from selling that bad horse
Than he made from all of the other horses he had.
"Tú no tienes sangre en el ojo,
You have no blood in your eye," said his brother.
"Cómo chingaste,
How you chingared that poor man
Who knew nothing about horses."
"Mira, hermano,
Look, my brother," said the horsetrader,
"Mientras que haya pendejos hay que chingarlos.
For as long as there are people like hanging pubic hairs,
We've got to keep on chingarin' them."

—Voice of ROBERTO ESPINOSA

To the East

A Texas Truck Driver

"Now this gauge here is your front air-tank pressure,"
The cattle truck driver says. "And this gauge here is your rear air-tank.
This here's your engine retarder, use it kinda like a brakin' device,
Like when you're goin' off a mountain.
If you push down and let off and pump just your brakes,
You'll catch your brakes on fire.
Over here's your pyrometer.
Here's your internal engine temperature gauge.
Here's your amp gauge, oil pressure gauge,
Water temperature, and manifold pressure.
That's the amount of air you're pullin' through your turbos.
Then you have your air cleaner pounds per inch gauge.
How much air you're pullin' through these air cleaners.
Then you got your glow plug. That's a little heater
In the tip of each injector that heats up diesel fuel for cold starts.
And a'course, you got your tachometer and speedometer.
The lever here slides the weight
Backward or forward on the fifth wheel.
Back towards the trailer or forward towards the cab.
For wet roads you move it to the front.
For easy ridin', I move it to the back.
And that, right there, is the interaxle differential lock trailer brake.
I almost got killed three years ago
On snow and ice when that thing didn't work.
I was in the hospital for two-and-a-half months.
A woman in a car pulled out in front of me.
I seen she had two little kids in the back of that car.
If it had justa been one woman,
I might have gone ahead and run over her,
But seein' those kids made me turn my truck
Over and run into the side of the bridge.
Broke my right arm, my right leg, split my skull,
Shattered my jaw and broke four fingers."
Drum sees a swollen place on his leg.

"Is that a part of the accident?" Drum asks.
"No, that's where a rattlesnake bit me," he says.
"I was in a sleepin' bag and they poured
  About fifty rattlesnakes in on top of me.
  Now a snake, he'll strike at heat and movement,
  But he won't strike at one without the other."
"How did you get out of that sleeping bag?" Drum asks.
"Mighty slow," he says, "mighty slow.
I rodeoed some, rode bareback broncs and clowned a little.
  Did a little stock car draggin',
  And hang glidin', but none of them things
  Was near as excitin' as gettin'
  Out of that sleepin' bag with fifty rattlesnakes."
"And what's this for?" Drum asks, pointing
  To a little lace maroon garter hanging over the mirror.
"That's to gauge a man's blood pressure," he says,
"And a'course to help keep it up."
  A cowgirl comes by, looks all around
  The rippled brown upholstery inside the truck.
"Hey, this is pretty neat," she says.
"I think I want to be a truck driver. Do you think I could?"
"How long can you stay awake?" he asks her.
"Oh, about twelve hours," she says.
"Well, he says, "that's how long you can be a truck driver."
  We beam the lights of two other trucks
  Onto a corral chock full of calves,
  Load 'em up in the darkness,
  The shadows of their running legs in the pickup truck lights.
  Finish up about two o'clock in the morning.
  The truck driver gets into the cab of the cattle truck.
"You boys need a drink?" he says.
  Puts his cattle hot-shot behind the seat.
  Gives us some water and cookies,
  Revs his big diesel engine up,
  Slides her into gear, goes laughing,
  Roaring away, laughing down the dirt road.
  Good old laughin' loco Texas truck driver.

How to Know

A One-Calf-a-Day Ropin' Mare

Well, Clay Lynch brought two horses out to the ranch.
One was a good-looking seven-year-old bay mare,
The other was a palomino gelding.
He wanted to sell 'em.
They didn't have any papers.
We didn't know if they were stolen.
We didn't know where they came from.
And Clay had spent a little time in the *calabozo* jail.
We were trying 'em out for rope horses.
Clay had rodeoed on 'em all Summer long.
"Now this bay mare," Clay says,
"She's a-goin' so good and doin' things so right,
You just maybe ought to rope,
Maybe, one calf a day on her, to keep her in practice.
And you don't want to drag any steers on her at all.
It'll ruin her good stop for calf ropin'."
Well, we tried those horses out and hauled them
Over to Chuck Beheney, the Bisbee vet,
To see if he could turn up something we hadn't seen.
"Well," he said, "I don't know where Clay got her
But she's sure a fine lookin', well-bred mare.
I imagine she can come out of a ropin' box pretty quick and stop,
But without any papers, all you've got here
Is a well-trained, unregistered, wind-broke mare.
I think she might hold up for you to rope
Maybe one calf a day on her,
And I don't think she could drag steers at all.
Yep, she's just about what Clay said she was,
An unregistered, wind-broke, one-calf-a-day-ropin' mare."
Ah, horse trading.

Truth

A Friendship

"Wiley, I need a horse for the kids to ride,
  To run barrels and poles and to learn to rope," says Drum.
"Well," says Wiley, "there's a pretty good sorrel horse
  That lives just down the road,
  And I tried to buy him." Wiley says,
"But your friend, Bill Bryan, kept passin' by.
  He said he'd give a thousand dollars for that horse,
  So the price of that horse kept goin' up."
  Drum asks his old friend, Bill Bryan, a few weeks later,
"Did you offer a thousand dollars
  For that gentle sorrel horse on Frontier Road?"
"I wouldn't give a thousand dollars for NO horse," Bill Bryan says.
"You watch that old Wiley,
  He's countin' on our friendship.
  He figures if he tells you I'd give a thousand dollars,
  He'll get more out of you.
  In three or four weeks he'll be a-tryin' to sell you that horse."
  About a month later at a ropin', Wiley comes walkin' up.
"Well, Drum, I bought that sorrel horse you was askin' about," he says,
"But I sure had to give a lot to get him.
  Your friend, Bill Bryan, kept passin' by and the price kept goin' up."
"Ah, Wiley, you've been caught by that same old friendship
  You were counting on to sell."
"Don't think any more, or any less of him for it," Bill Bryan says to Drum,
"That's horse tradin'."

—Voice of BILL BRYAN

An Eye for Horses and Men

The Penitentiary

Well, Billy Brown and Drum went to try out
A blue horse on a neighbor's ranch.
Rode him around the arena a couple of times,
Asked the price.
"If I had the money, I'd buy him," said Billy.
"I wouldn't quibble about two or three hundred dollars."
So we bought that horse for a pretty high price.
Took him home to Guadalupe Canyon.
Billy rode him for three months.
"This horse ought to be worth all the other horses
You've got on this ranch," Billy said.
But he was a "head throwin',
Stargazin' son of a gun" three months later,
When Billy got done ridin' him up and down the canyon.
So we rode him pretty hard and regular
For another ten months or so.
Showed him to Bill Bryan one day in the Spring.
Spun him around in little circles, figure-eighted him,
And had him near lopin' backwards, but really,
Couldn't seem to get him to do things right.
"I don't know what it is about him," Drum said to Bill.
"I keep working with him,
Hoping someday he'll come around.
He'd sure make a top rope horse,
Or a barrel, or a pole horse for the kids.
What do you think?
Have you ever seen a horse with that much action before?"
"The penitentiary is full of guys with good action," Bill says.
"Better look there into his eyes,
That's where you'll see what counts."

—Voice of BILL BRYAN

Social Status

How to Be High Class

"I seen Pete Pasco a-struttin' around,
  Actin' like he was a high-class big shot
  With a bunch of them cow buyers," said Bud Robertson.
"I thought to myself, 'Why, I'll fix you, Pete.'
  So I said, 'Goddamn, Pete, did you
  Come in here with your spurs on?'
  'Why, hell no,' said Pete.
  'Oh, I'm sorry,' I said, 'must be them goddamn goat turds
  A-rattlin' around in your boots.'"

Holdin' the Herd till the Buyer Comes

Nothin' to do, but sit here and wait …
Warner comes ridin' past.
"Kelly and me better go to the corrals
And see what's holdin' 'em up," he says.
Sunlight tremblin' on the tumbleweed
Startin' to get brown in October.
"I think these cows and calves are straight,"
Warner says, "No doubt there's a few crossed up,
But we gotta give old Everett Campbell
Somethin' to do when he comes."
Springtime, and the rains are a long ways away.
Old Cacahuate rubs his bridle against his leg.
The light and the wind tremble
Through the soft dun hair along his mane.
Nothin' to do but sit here and wait …

• • • • •

TURQUOISE STONES IN THE CREEK BED ...
       THE SOUND OF THE HORSE'S HOOVES IN THE SAND.

WHITE LIGHTNIN' PASSIN' THROUGH

Short, coupled muscles bulging under his shirt,
Tough and tanned, cap with a brim that says Alcatraz Café.
A pipe set in his mouth at evening when he stops work.
He sits with a glass of Wild Turkey whiskey
And thinks about each day that passed.
Then up again and gone before five in the morning.
A jack of all trades.

A Jack of All Trades

I. A Giddy Up and a Whoa and a Catskinner

"Goddamn, how the hell are you?" the catskinner yells,
   Roaring with his one-ton truck, off the hill and into the canyon.
"The brakes went out, almost went over a cliff.
   Air compressor tryin' to kill my ass.
   Fuel trailer tryin' to kill my ass.
   Hell, I'll be buried under one of these blackjack oaks.
   Paid one hundred seventy-five dollars
   For a brand new generator for the bulldozer,
   But the son-of-a-bitchin' generator don't work.
   Fixin' one is worse than a goddamn chicken,
   Pickin' his teeth with a paper toothpick.
   Goddamn sorry-assed piece of shit,
   If anything kills me, it's gonna be that heap of scrap metal.
   Hell, you trust the hydraulics to hold up her blade,
   She'll cover your ass in a heartbeat.
   Havin' a bulldozer is about as close to havin' a wife as you can get.
   Spend every last cent you got on her,
   Eats like hell, keeps you exhausted all the time,
   Breaks you on the fuel bill, and runs around hotter'n hell all day.
   Let's shut this son of a bitch down and take a break."

II. A Fairy Tale

I guess a fairy tale begins, "Once upon a time."
A sea story begins, "Now this ain't no bullshit."
Now this ain't no bullshit,
The Navy spent ten thousand dollars transportin' me all over the world and back—
Yokosuka, Sasebo, Kobe, Hong Kong, Singapore, Kuala Lumpur, Malaysia,
Hiroshima, where the bomb exploded,
Statue of Eternal Peace with his hand standin' up in the air.
What were those countries like? What did we see, what did we do?
First, we went to the red-light houses, then we got drunk,
Then we went back to the red-light houses again,
Always were old places of eternal peace.
Hell, we'd come into port with six hundred dollars in our pockets, a-hollerin',
Flap, fight, or run a footrace, we're tin-can sailors.
Them Chinese girls there ain't built like these girls here.
Firm small titties with just about three hairs a-stickin' out.
Lookin' back, we ate a lotta of T-bone steaks in a lotta ports.
And a lotta over-easy eggs in a lotta ports.
Saw a lotta bottoms in a lotta ports.
And we definitely caused inflation at the flap houses.
Then we'd come back to the States after six months at sea.
We'd find our loved ones, just like we'd left them, happy and freshly flapped.

III. Haulin' Ass in the Springtime

"Now I'm thirty-nine years old.
I've been in every state in the union,
But I ain't never yet decided what I'm gonna do with my life."
Leonard Maddux said, "You'd better hurry or you're gonna be dead soon.
You're gonna kill yourself and go straight to the devil."
"Hell," says the catskinner, "the devil thinks he's got troubles now,
He ain't had no trouble at all till I get down there.
Well, I worked in a Chinese laundry,
Then I worked diggin' graves,
When I got done diggin' 'em, I worked fillin' 'em in.

Lived in a mausoleum, swept the son of a bitch out,
Wiped out the cobwebs, the corpse didn't mind.
I probably made her feel at home, camping out in her mausoleum.
Date said 1881. She probably died campin' out too.
I didn't know who I was sleepin' with. Sometimes, it's better that way.
It wasn't too bad for a while,
But just about the time you was restin' good in that mausoleum,
There'd be three or four guys die.
Sorry bastards, never die when you want 'em to.
They paid me a dollar an hour, room and no board.
Twenty or thirty mausoleums in that graveyard.
Had to find my own room.
Colder'n a bitch all Winter,
Can't dig the ground till Spring.
That's one reason, boy, I hauled ass around Springtime.
They don't believe in none of this backhoe shit."

IV. Workin' with the Dead

When you're dead, you're a-layin' by yourself.
Throw the dirt in on top of the box, everybody cryin' all over the place.
I waited and waited for everybody to go,
So's I could throw the dirt in.
Got to be a husband there, or a boyfriend.
"You the husband?" I'd ask. Boyfriend, close relative.
Anyway, he stayed when everybody else left.
It was colder'n hell. I wanted to get back to build a fire,
Warm up that mausoleum, relax.
"Buddy," I told him, "You just sit there
And visit with her and you guys can talk.
I'll shovel the dirt in quiet."
Hell, for a dollar an hour,
I'da shoveled that son of a bitch in too.
Rich. Had a hell of a nice block of rock,
Big old gravestone, the size of a tree.
They wanted you to set up those goddamn gravestones by yourself.
I couldn't see no future in it for me, so I quit.

Went to work in a morgue.
   They asked what credentials I had.
"Credentials?" I told 'em,
"Hell, I've been workin' with the dead for three months.
   But wages wasn't too high. I had to move in with 'em."

V. Gettin' Your Ass Fired

Well I only lasted in that morgue for two weeks,
Dead bodies a-layin' all over the place.
So I trucked on down the road and got me a job as a chauffeur.
Worked for a millionaire.
That was a pretty good job, but they had a bell in your room.
That bell got to me. When they rung that goddamn bell,
Your ass better be flyin' out there in shining armor.
One or two in the morning,
Those girls would want to go somewhere.
I lasted a month. I told that millionaire,
"Sir, your wife and daughters is drivin' me nuts."
He said, "Hell boy, welcome to the club."
Then I drove trucks, hauled feed, hauled milk, ran cranes,
Worked as a mechanic, worked as a welder. I was hurtin' for food.
You live on one soda a day, or if you're lucky sometimes, one soda a half a day.
You punch that Coke machine and you get a Coke for fifteen cents.
Then for dinner, you could get cheese and crackers,
And that was your other ten cents.
Worked as a shoe salesman. I couldn't take that job, neither.
Hell, try on thirty-five more pairs of shoes.
Jesus, stores are hard to work in,
'Cause you can't tell the customers to stuff it up their ass.
Some woman sat there for two hours,
Tried on every goddamn shoe in the place.
Finally, I told her, "If you want to see anymore of those goddamn shoes,
Get your ass up there and look."
I headed for the back of the store,
To tell the store manager I quit,
But she beat me to him and he fired my ass.

VI. White Lightnin'

Then I worked milkin' cows,
Worked on a pig farm, worked on a chicken farm,
Lived with an old lady who had eight goats,
Lived with this girl, Agnes, who had five boyfriends.
They never knew I was in the house.
It wasn't too bad, but it was a little risky.
Thought about pullin' a holdup
In this dinky-ass town in Ohio, Chillicothe.
When you're hungry and cold, a gun can get you what you need.
From the womb to the tomb,
From the erection to the resurrection,
It's insurance. You're in good hands, just like Allstate.
It's better for the Law to catch you with it,
Than for the boys to catch you without it.
You're dead if you don't, and you're dead if you do.
If anybody's goin' to be lyin' to the coroner, make sure it's you.
Better to be sittin' in front of a jury of twelve,
Than bein' carried to the grave by six.
That's the way it was, movin' West.
Some of 'em made it, and some of 'em didn't.
Well then, I thought I had better be a cross-country trucker.
I never did drive that truck no faster than she'd go neither,
But that truckin', it's for the birds.
It's better to be a cowboy.
Get on your own jackass or a horse,
Go on up in the mountains,
You don't need no paperwork, no gas stations, no turn signals, no roads,
No stop lights, no driver's license, no haulin' papers, no invoices.
Don't need no nothin', just a giddy up and a whoa.
Pass me that bottle, don't homestead the son of a bitch.
So long, I'll see you at the big roundup, that is, if you can make it.
You and me, we're white lightnin', passin' through.

—*Voice of* DICK STOFF

Modern Literature

Portrait of a Poet by His Friend the Catskinner, January 18, 1975

In Drum's mind he hears,
"Old rains come down softly,
Thunder and clouds bring my loves to me ..."
But he hears Dick say,
"Drum, wherefore hast thou put the oil for the bulldozer?
Jesus Christ, I hope we ain't a-gonna sit around
And write poems all day.
We ain't gonna get nothin' done, which brings us back to
Where'd you put the goddamn hydraulic oil?
What?
You forgot to get it when you went to town?
Listen to me.
Just get a piece of cardboard or carry some cotton around with you.
Whichever ear you hear good in,
Put the cotton and the cardboard in the other ear,
So then, what I tell you don't go out the other side.
Hell, they're goin' to put you away in a house soon,
They're goin' to be arms huggin' you,
They're goin' to be your own.
What the hell you got there?
Do you carry a saddlebag in your pants leg?
A canteen in one boot,
A bottle of Wild Turkey whiskey in the other.
Hell, you're better than a goddamn kangaroo."

—Voice of DICK STOFF

Modern Conveniences

The Catskinner and the Washing Machine

"Give it a kick in the right corner," he yells,
"It's a sensitive machine, it needs a little initiative.
 OK, first thing, have you checked the fuses?"
"No," says Drum, "it can't be the fuses."
"Look, I start at the top and work my way down," he says,
"I'm not like you poets who start at the bottom and
 Then try to work your way up."
 Drum starts to write all this down.
"Get out of here, poet!" yells the catskinner.
 Bang, bang, kicks the machine.
"Goddamn we need less poets here and more workers."
 Humm. The machine starts.
"Whatever you want to do, do it," yells the catskinner.
"Let's try rinse." Bang.
"If there's a short and I light up, you'll know I found it.
 Ouch, goddamn, I found it.
 Just grab in those wires," says the catskinner.
"The life you save may be your own,
 It'll end your poetry and you'll be the greatest light this side of Douglas.
 What you need is a good old-fashioned washin' machine,
 One that you can see. You can put in your clothes and see 'em.
 Run 'em through that wringer.
 Let me explain it to you. Look, that automatic washin' machine.
 That water's soakin' up the dirt.
 In comes the fresh water.
 All that fresh water's soakin' up the dirt,
 That dirt goes right through your clothes again
 While it's goin' right down the drain.
 Get a wringer washer, you'll live longer.
 Just grab the lever, pull on the throttle,
 Turn the crank and that son of a gun, she takes off,
 Washin' and wringin' clothes like she's goin' out of style.
 Didn't I ever tell you a poet should never work on a washing machine?

The Lord didn't put shade down for havin' it fall on the ground.
He put it down for havin' it fall on one of you goddamn poets!
Now, you gotta buy a new motor for this washing machine.
She just blew up
BANG!
That's all she wrote."

—Voice of DICK STOFF

How to Write a Book

"Quit Writin' Everythin' True."

"This story between you and me
  Goes a long way back," says the catskinner,
"You should of wrote your memoirs.
  Shit, you should write them now.
  Shit, you don't get nowhere writin' those goddamn poems.
  Shit, ain't hardly nobody can understand 'em
  Unless he's drunk a half bottle of whiskey.
  That's cause you're writin' 'em true all the time.
  That's bullshit. Nobody wants to read the truth.
  Give 'em fiction, that's what they want.
  You got to have a cowboy takin' a shit under a tree ...
  But that's Montana, that's not around here,
  Cause there ain't hardly no trees here in this desert country,
  And he hears a growlin' like this,
'Grrr grrr,' and a big old grizzly with claws about a foot long
  Comes and creases his ass with those claws,
  And then that wound gets infected,
  And the mother#$%er's gonna die except, unless,
  For a beautiful woman, who comes along,
  And nurses him back to life.
  The only thing is, she don't like cowboys,
  So, that's where the romance part comes in.
  You gotta give people excitement, blood, guts,
  Somebody's ass ripped by a grizzly.
  I'll buy ten books of that shit.
  That's what people believe in.
  You can't give em,
      'The sun is shinin' on the rocks
      And the wind is blowin'
      And we're started out early in the mornin'
      And when we hit the cattle,
      They ain't gonna move,
      They just wanna drag ass down the canyon.'

Who the hell wants to read that shit?
But with these environmentalists today,
You never can tell, it might sell,
Cause if you don't kiss the air and you don't kiss the ground ...
If you don't fight for the bottom ... that's the whales,
And you don't fight for the middle ...
That's the grizzlies and the wolves,
And you don't fight for the top ...
That's those big condor buzzard bastards,
The bald eagles, and the goddamn moon.
Ain't hardly a soul exceptin' a few astronauts ever been there
So why the hell worry about protectin' it?
But hell, a guy readin' your poems could go to sleep
And fall off the hay mound where he's settin'
And break his arm and sue you.
You got to put some fast-ridin', ass-bustin', shit-eatin' shit
In the first chapter, right off, and it's gotta be wrote
So every lowly son of a bitch like me can understand it right off.
And quit writin' everythin' that's true all the time.
When somebody's writin' in the dark,
And he can't see what he's writin', he's crazy.
I'm sayin' that because you can't see a goddamn thing you're writin'.
I can't even see your hand and you're writin'.
You're writin' and you're crazy.
Your mind's out ahead of your body.
All you got to do when your mind gets out like that
Is get a 'come along' or a fence-stretcher,
And just winch that son of a bitch right back in.
If you knew you were crazy, it would be different,
But you're still tryin' to be a nice, normal person.
You don't seem crazy, but you are crazy.
The only thing is, you don't have bars on your window
And like some woman said, you're free.
Pass me that bottle, don't homestead that son of a bitch."

—Voice of DICK STOFF

· · · · ·

TURQUOISE STONES IN THE CREEK BED ...
THE SOUND OF THE HORSE'S HOOVES IN THE SAND.

THE TRACKERS

Along the Trail

We, the hunters, came to follow the trail of the calf-killing lion.
We struck his track in a draw, South of Animas Pass.
In places, there were tracks in the sands to follow.
In places, the damp sands in the arroyos were frozen.
During the night, the lion headed North.
We left the ranch headquarters, way before sunup.
In the canyons when the sands thawed,
There was no scent or track to follow.
Here now, high on this mountain rim,
Beneath these green rock lichen cliffs,
We have a long way to ride,
Back across these deep canyons, and a longer way,
To know how to come home.

Lion

I. The Grasses Spring Back

"Tú siempre quieres ver toda la huella,
  You always want to see the whole track," Roberto says.
"Look where the grass has only bent a little,
  Or a pebble's moved.
Look where something has scratched across the sand.
Then, when you lose the track, you always look too far away,
Away from that place where you lost the track.
Look close, where the grass seems changed,
  Or where a pebble's rolled.
The mare's track, where it crossed
Through the grass, was easy to follow,
Because her weight broke the grass stems.
A lion's pad only bends the stems down.
The grasses spring back up again.
You need to become the lion, crossing on the trail,
  Then the track is clear."

—*Voice of* ROBERTO ESPINOSA

What the Earth Has Imagined

II. The Lion's Paw

An old lion will stay in the country he knows.
The deer he needs to eat are all around him.
He is like the Indian who plucks the song
He will live by,
  from the air ...
All it takes is *mucho ojo,*
Much eye to see, much ear to hear,
To follow what the Earth has imagined.
Hay que ser la pata del león ...
Be the lion's paw pressing the leaves into the earth,
  Then the print is clear.

—*Voice of* ROBERTO ESPINOSA

III. A Cow

A cow's bawling echoes from the rocky cliffs above us.
Mooooooooooo, moooooooooooo,
Come on, little Bayleaf colt,
Let's climb up through those rocks and ledges,
To see what's going on up there by the cliffs.
A wide-horned cow, struttin' a bag, her head held high.
She's nervous, and on the prod.
Her milk bag big, the teats swollen out.

IV. The Tracks

"*Allí van las huellas,* there go the tracks," says Roberto.
He gets off his palomino,
Ties his pack horse to an oak tree, to be afoot,
To start following the cow's track
Back to where she came from.
The bawling echoes from the cliff.
Moooooooo, moooooooo,
Echoes around the rims of the canyon.
We prowl over the ledges,
To tell if a lion has killed the cow's calf,
Drug it off, and hidden it to eat a part later.
Near dusk, Roberto finds a trace of the drag.
"*Mira el arrastre,*" he says.
"The lion killed the calf by this *quijote* stalk.
I saw the cow looking here.
Here, the lion waited for the calf,
By those rocks he sprang."

—*Voice of* ROBERTO ESPINOSA

V. Flecks of Water

See the claw marks in the sand,
Urrrrr qué grande el cabrón,
A brown calf's leg under the *sacahuista* leaves,
Oak and *algerita* cover him up.
Ah, the lion hasn't eaten yet, we just scared him away.
Come on, little Bayleaf, two-year old colt,
Let's light out for the ranch.
We'll need some help to catch this calf-killing lion.
Quit teetering along the edge of these rocky cliff ledges,
Rocks sliding off into the air,
Or you or me, neither of us, is goin' to get back home tonight.
Duck those branches, now watch that low limb in the trail.
Along the arroyo, white flecks of water in the moonlight
Drift past ... away on the stream.

VI. At Morning

"There he goes," calls Warner Glenn.
A lion's pad mark by the white gravelly sand.
One oak leaf, drifting on the rim of the blue sky above us.
The broken canyons stretching far off below.
Warner leads his mule along a ledge.
The mule sets back.
The trail's too rough.
He tilts his nose up into the air.
Lion dogs go running past him on the trail.
Kink and Molly, *Ooouuuurrh, Ooouuuurrh,*
Susie, Jaws, Speck, and Smokey, *Ooooouuuurrh.*
"Is that a lion bark, or is that a bullshit bark?" laughs Warner.
Roberto comes riding by.
He's been out here in these mountains a couple of weeks.
He's ready to head for town.
"Estos perros son como los vaqueros entrados a la Zona,

These lion dogs are like *vaqueros*," he says,
"Who follow an old trail,
Into the red-light houses in Agua Prieta."

—*Voices of* WARNER GLENN *and* ROBERTO ESPINOSA

VII. Late Afternoon

Early evening after climbing the cliffs,
Sliding down through the brush,
Tracking and riding all day,
Kreeeeeeee, kreeeeeeeeee,
Two red-tailed hawks, screaming above the box canyon,
The sound of the waters passing,
Shusssh, the sound of the wind blowing,
High on the cliff rims, ruffling in the lion's fur,
Arrgrr the lion jumps, just misses Roberto,
The crack of a shot echoes from the cliffs.
One oak leaf falling,
Drops into the canyon below,
A light wind blows it above the creek water,
Old leaves drift past, away on that stream.

TURQUOISE STONES IN THE CREEK BED ...
THE SOUND OF THE HORSE'S HOOVES IN THE SAND.

THE TRAPPERS

A track made on top of the frost
Will stay until the frost is gone.
A scent left on the rocks when there's been a dew
Will be gone away in Summer, by the middle of morning.

A Covered Set for a Lion

I. A Number Four-and-a-Half Steel Trap

Huckleberry colt waits, tied to a mesquite.
Shakes himself.
Drum hears the shovel, tied to the saddle, clank.
The clanking dies away.
Old big-pawed lion, you've killed seven calves this Spring.
By Cloverdale Peaks, three more are missing.
This lion's like an old lofer wolf.
He don't come back nor cover his kills.
A lion, he'll eat the heart and the liver first.
A bobcat, he'll eat the ears and the brisket
That's on a calf or a deer he mighta killed himself.
A wolf, he'll work on the quarters.
Scoop out a place here in the dirt and the sand,
In a hollow between three cedar trees.
Zzzz aaahh zzzz ooo aaahhh
The green flies buzz,
They whisper away through the pale caves,
In the dead calf's stomach.
Walter's two boots rocking on the springs of the trap.
Pull back the trap jaws,
A number four-and-a-half steel trap,
Trigger set thumb back.
Fingers underneath the trip,

So if the jaws spring, you ought to get away.
One of Lucille Taylor's relatives made a bear set.
Got both hands caught.
They found him in the Springtime,
Chained to a pine tree up in the Blue Country.
Tie a link of the chain of one steel trap
By a piece of bailing wire to the link of another.

II. Not to Give Away Anything Too Soon

Pack the dirt firm by the edge of the jaws,
So the earth won't give away anything too soon.
A hollow place between three cedar trees,
A piece of burlap sack over the hollow,
And the jaws of the trap.
Old cedar needles, rolled in your hands,
Drop from your hands, roll on the burlap.
Tiny pebbles flipped off with a light cedar twig,
Ping in the rocks, ricochet through the leaves.
A hollow place between three cedar trees.
Huckleberry colt thinks it's getting pretty late
To do any more work today,
Stretches out and pees.
He and me wait here to keep the buzzards
Off the traps, by the bait, till the sunlight's gone away.
Our scent from a shower while we made our set
Will stay unless it rains again.
The mother cow bawls low in her throat,
For her calf who won't get up again.
The green flies are stuffed, and buzz and whisper
Away through the pale caves in the dead calf's stomach.
Zzz ooo aaahhh zzz ooo aaahhh
A seashell sound,
A fly in your ear.
Guess there's nothin' more to do,
But brush out our tracks,
And back out of here and go.

• • • • •

With thanks to Walter Ramsey and Marvin and Warner Glenn for chasing the lion and telling a poem.

The Tongue of the Lion

I. Going Home

Here, high on this mountain rim,
Beneath these green rock lichen cliffs,
I am an old grey lion, lying
Along the thin, clawed bark of a twisted cedar limb.
Slobber and saliva hang from my lips.
My right ear is in tatters,
My chest has white scars,
My left leg has bite marks from the teeth of a jaguar.
The howling black and tan hounds have bayed me.
The canyons stretch away below,
The arroyos, the yellow grass valleys,
The mesas, the distant blue mountain ranges.
I hear the sound of the hunters' voices,
They look for me among the lichen ledges, the piñon limbs.
Their grey mules' shod hooves
Click towards me, over the arroyo rocks and the sands.
Now the hunters are tying their mules
Onto the low oak brush, below my limb.
The curved tails of the black and tan hounds are wagging.
Their howling echoes from the ledge-covered cliffs.
Now they come to kill me.

II. The Quick Knives

The gun, a stick, is pointed towards me.
I feel the quick bullet as the rush of a wind,
Ruffling through the light grey hair of my fur.
It drives past deepness, into the throbbing,
The grey-muscled meat of my heart.
I fall, I fall. The hounds' teeth grab my skin,
My eyes glaze, but I am gone.
Then my lion spirit lifts from this rim rock ledge,
From this last cedar limb, where I have been waiting.
But then, with their quick knives, when they slit
Into the soft fur above my heart and pull away the skin,
They will see the lithe lines of the limbs,
And the lines of each sinew will be clear,
And the blue mountain ranges,
And the long desert valleys,
The canyon deer, and the peaks,
And the snows, within my skin.
Where were they going, when they came to kill me?

—Voice of the Lion

The Devil's Hole

A Silver Thread

It seems like they'd have to be crazy to go up that windin' canyon,
But we'll go over there and check.
'Cause when it gets real dry in June like it is now,
Cattle will start a-follerin' that little silver thread.
A cow brute, she always wants to drink
Right where the water's fresh and cool and just a-pourin' out,
Cows and horses both.
I guess maybe people, too.
Philip McDonald's best horse trailed that tricklin' thread.
He first saw it where it was a-runnin' down into the pool.
The sunlight comin' off of the water there, was maybe playin'
In the shadows on those cliffs, above the pools,
And the water was a-drippin' down off of the rock.
When they found him, he was dead, starved by the spring.
He'd followed that silver thread all the way back up from the pool,
Back to the place where the water came from.
When he turned around and he looked back the way he'd come,
Just looked so scary to him, he never could come back out.
We'll ride over there and check. We'll cut some cedar limbs,
Throw 'em across the openin' between those cliffs,
So these little yearlin' calves won't take that trail.
Where that silver thread's a-shinin', and then disappears,
To leave a critter alone,
Rimmed up high, by those pools above the rock,
They call that dang place the Devil's Hole.
And those red-winged butterflies
Are the only things can go in over the sharp rock and come back out.
Them and the lions, and those mournin' doves a-hollerin'
Coo-COO, coo, coo, coo, across those pools, way up high in the canyon.
Some trails, a horse or a cow brute had better not follow to the end.

—Voice of WALTER RAMSEY

TURQUOISE STONES IN THE CREEK BED ...
        THE SOUND OF THE HORSE'S HOOVES IN THE SAND.

INDIANS

Singing Winds

These are food for your spirit to eat,
Sunlight playing on the dusty grass,
Light rain falling on the sycamore leaves,
Dropping into the drifting sand,
Blowing, drifting, away.

Borrowing

A Bull

Walter Ramsey was camped down Guadalupe Canyon.
He was taking care of thirty-nine head of cows
For his old schoolmate, Stella Luz.
"I guess I'll have to buy a bull to get these cows bred,"
Stella said to Walter one Wintertime day.
But Walter knew she didn't have the money to do it.
"Well, I been a-managin' for a bull,"
He said to her one day in the Springtime.
In the Summertime, Stella's neighbor, John Magoffin,
Come a-drivin' along the canyon road in his little red jeep.
Them kids of his was afoot, a-drivin' a gentle black bull
Back down to John's country in the lower part of the canyon.
"Goddamn, there he goes," says Walter Ramsey,
"Everything I do is wrong."
"Did you put that black bull of John's in my pasture?"
Stella asks Walter Ramsey.
"No," lies Walter, so you can't even see his heart,
Just a-twinklin' there somewhere,
Way down in the depths of those part Texas Indian,
Old Texas Indian brown eyes.

Walter Ramsey brings
The three Borderland cultures together,
That of the Spanish, the Indian, and the white,
And the further mixtures of them all.
He brings them together in his own blood,
Part Indian and part white, and that of his wife,
Raquel, part Spanish and part white,
And speaks of a plant in three different languages.
He tells the story about his uncle Stewart Hunt and some missing horses.
"Stewart was ranchin' in Mexico in the 1920s," says Walter.
"Stewart had been missin' horses for some time.
He thought maybe his Mexican neighbor was stealin' them.

But one day Stewart was lion huntin'
And his lion dogs treed an old Indian woman.
Stewart began to look around the camp
Where evidently she was stayin'.
He found some horse bones and he also found
One of his missing horses that he himself couldn't catch.
She had tied the horse to a tree by braiding together
A few of them leaves from a plant.
You know, that plant the Indians call *sacahuista*.
That's that plant the Mexicans call *palmilla*,
That the white men call "bear grass."
She had been eatin' Stewart's horses.
Stewart said he couldn't figure out
How she caught them or how she killed them
Because all she had was a sharp stick.
She must have not been able to travel
With that last band of Apaches who were
Still runnin' in them Sierra Madres till the 1930s."
So, it is there, on Walter's tongue,
That the three different cultures
Of Borderlands people
Are brought together.

The Moon in the Water

Everisto and Drum were walking along the irrigated field.
The killdeer flying up through the dusk light,
Three chickens missing,
Gone from the ocotillo rib chicken coop.
They were prowling around, looking for tracks.
"Allí están las huellas, there," says Everisto.
The trail of a coon crossing
Through the moonlight in a puddle of water.
"Ya yo sé lo que voy a hacer,
Now I know what I'll do," says Everisto.
"I'll set a trap for the coon in the water,
Y cuando viene el watepi, and when the coon comes,
He won't be able to see the trap.
Va a ver no más que la luna en el agua.
He'll see no more than the moon in the water."

—*Voice of* EVERISTO WASICA, *Opata Indian, Hibeka the Hatchet*

Indian

So Quick, He Could Catch a Javelina Boar

We were horseback, a two-and-a-half-hour ride
From the canyon of the Guadalupe Ranch headquarters.
We met Don Josecito, coming up the country from Mexico.
He was afoot. He was looking for work.
We told him to come with us, that we had work for him to do.
The country was very broken—
Don Josecito chose to take a different trail than we did with our horses.
He arrived at the ranch well before we did.
I told this to Alfredo Bernal.
He told me Don Josecito was very quick on his feet.
"*La gente*, the people say he is *tan ligero*,
He is so quick, that he can catch a javelina boar."
I told Don Josecito, thinking what Alfredo had said would please him.
"*Fíjate*, imagine that," said Don Josecito,
"Imagine they say this about me,
Me, who does not want to be called an Indian."
Then he told a story about a huge lion
That had been stalking him in the dusk light,
As he came up to his camp.
In the morning light he looked and he saw
The lion's pad marks on top of his own footprints.
During a snowstorm, Laddie Pendelton found
Don Josecito huddled below a cutbank,
Trying to build a little fire to keep warm.
Laddie took Don Josecito home with him to the Cloverdale Ranch.
Over the next few days that they were together,
Don Josecito told Laddie of his life.
Don Josecito was somewhere above seventy years old,
As near as he could figure.
But of course, in those days, there were no records kept
Of when an Indian was born or died.
After telling the story of his life for a few days,
Don Josecito became quiet.

"Well, and then what happened?" Laddie asked.
"*Pues*, well," said Don Josecito,
"*Estuvimos civilizados,* then we became civilized."

—*Voices of* LADDIE PENDLETON, ALFREDO BERNAL, *and* DON JOSECITO

To Be of the Earth

A Flame

The gringos, North of the border,
Call this low yellow-flowered,
Woody-stemmed plant "snakeweed"
Because its existence as a weed
Is of no more account than the existence of a snake.
Cattle cannot eat snakeweed,
Its presence in abundance
Is an indication of overgrazing.
Only the snakes live where it lives.
But the Mexican *vaqueros* of Indian background
Call this same low-lying flowered plant *Tata Lencho*.
They speak of it with reverence.
They say, *"Después de Dios, Tata Lencho,*
Just after God there is Grandfather Lorenzo."
When they have been riding
During a cold time of the year,
When they themselves can no longer
Endure that cold astride their horses' backs,
When their fingers have become so numb
They are unable to feel the reins,
When they can barely open or close the buttons on their flies,
Then they stiffly step down from their horse's backs
In the early morning light of Fall,
Or later in Winter, in the rain or the snow,
They search for this low-lying
Yellow-flowered weed to start a fire,

To warm their numbed hands and chilled bodies.
They smile when the match flame begins
To move through the yellow flowered twigs
They say, *"Después de Dios, Tata Lencho,*
After God, Grandfather Lorenzo."

The Fate of Civilization

Echoes

The *vaquero* says, *"Los viejitos,*
The oldest men who lived there,
Tell that sometimes they hear
The sounds of Indian drums and old men chanting.
Of course, *no puede ser más que los ecos,*
You know they can't be
Hearing anything but echoes
That have been left there,
From the drums beating near those old rocks.
Y lógicamente, and logically,
Since civilization, you know those echoes
Are getting harder and harder to hear
Because of the noises of trucks
On the paved streets,
And airplanes flying over these hills,
Y los escándalos de la gente,
And the scandals of the people."

The Ruins at Chichén Itzá

Civilizations, philosophies, religions,
Hearts thrown into the well,
Loves, wars, slaves, generals,
Captives, monuments, horses, gods,
Crosses, entrails, and gold,
Chichén Itzá, Uxmal, Tulum, Campeche,
Old rock, carved, tumbling ruins.
Copal, romero, albahaca smoke,
Blood on the stone, stained altars and the stones beneath.
Sunlight on the ruins, dark old rocks,
Places for laughing children to pee in.

Rafael Quijada
Sierra Madre, Sonora, México

Cuando el búho canta, el indio muere.
No es cierto, pero sucede.
When the owl calls, the Indian dies.
It is not certain, but it happens.

I go now to see my *cuñada, la que me repechó,*
She who took me to her bosom when my father was killed,
When my mother went to live with another man.
Now my *cuñada* is dying. She is not sick, but only old.
When she goes, we will place her body in a sack,
To bury her in the ground.
A sack or the mountain wind waits for me as well.
Even as I climb the steep cedar breaks,
I feel *calambres* in my legs.
Calambres are the pains when one walks,
When the nerves in the legs tighten.
I grow down and old, like the tail of the cow.
Someday I will not be able to go to find work
From the borderline as far as Pueblo Colorado.
When that time comes, I will need a *patrón,*
A boss who will not try only to *ganar,*
To win all he is able from my back and my hands.
I do not like the towns. In the mountains, the head is clear.
If I could stay in a *jacal,* a hut of bear grass, near the canyon spring,
We would wake in the mornings and walk to the ridgeline,
To look towards those blue valleys, and cradles of the Sierra Madre.
There I would remember those touches of my women,
The long circles, the roundups, the rock-footed horses I'd ridden.
There I would wait, to drift again,
With the Spring wind through these mountain passes.
There I would wait until the owl calls.

—Voice of RAFAEL QUIJADA

• • • • •

"Un caballo, un perro, un gato, es igual como uno,
  a horse, a dog, a cat, is the same as one," says Rafael,
"Hay que tratarlos con cariño,
  Each one must be treated with sweetness."

The Hopi People and the Christian Church

The Shortest Bridge in Shungopavi

"A long time ago," Coot-si-wii-kii-ooo-ma says,
"The Spanish came with the horses and the cows and the church
And they had Hopi men bring big logs from *Nu va tue qui ovi,*
The snow-capped San Francisco Peaks, to build the church in Hopi.
When the church was built, the priest sent a chief to *Tuf ka vey*
Grand Canyon, to bring back baptismal water.
But the chief, he didn't like the look of things,
He only went to the spring and then went back home to his wife.
When he came in the door of his house he looked in.
Saw the priest there on top of his wife,
That's when he began to think maybe some things should change.
About that time, runners came from Taos to the Hopi pueblos.
Each runner carried a rope with knots tied into the rope.
Each knot stood for a day, and beginning with the day the runner left,
Each day a knot was untied.
When the last knot was untied in Hopi, the Indian men rose up,
Killed the priest, the Christians, and even killed some of our own people.
They wiped them all out.
And that's the reason we still got a few Hopis left."

> —*Told by* COOT-SI-WII-KII-OOO-MA (DELBRIDGE HONANI),
> *4 feet 7 inches tall. He's the guy who carries a lot of people*
> *across to insight, the shortest "bridge" in Shungopavi.*

Chant for Coming Home

Hey Yo

Hey yo hey yo wittsee
Hey yo hey yo wittsee
Hey yo hey yo wittsee
Hey yo hey yo wittsee
Hey yo hey yo wittsee
Hey yo hey yo wittsee
Hey yo hey yo wittsee
Hey yea no way
Hey yea no way
A home in the rangelands,
A home in the creeks,
A home in the mountains, the dry arroyo sands,
A home on this Earth who we used to be,
A home that on Earth we used to be,
Mountains, creeks, deserts, arroyo sands,
A home from wherever we stand.
Hey yo hey yo wittsee
Hey yo hey yo wittsee
Hey yo hey yo wittsee
Hey yo hey yo wittsee
Hey yo hey yo wittsee
Hey yo hey yo wittsee
Hey yo hey yo wittsee
Hey yo hey yo wittsee
Hey yea no way
Where ever we came from,
Where ever we stand,
Where ever we go from here,
To the cedar breaks,
To the canyons,

To those cores of our hands shaped by the land.
Hey yo hey yo wittsee
Hey yo hey yo wittsee
Hey yo hey yo
Hey yea no way
Hea

—A Peyote Chant

The Navajos

In a Navajo, the wind is always blowing.
In the Navajo weaves, we hear you calling.
Old Navajo, now, who are you calling?
Across the dry mesas, these falling cliff sands,
Where he and she call to one another,
In the sweet touches of the raindrops,
The shy touch of your hand.
Now hear the sounds of the horses' hooves.
Now hear the sounds of the drums weaving.

Oklahoma

Gilbert Swiven Wilbert Jr., Quarter Chocktaw
American Airlines Flight, Arizona to Oklahoma City

"Well, I'm mostly in the contractin' business," he says.
"Mostly I work mostly for the Indians. Pretty good work.
But sometimes a little hard to get paid.
Last Spring, we had to drill holes
In the tribe's safety deposit box to get our money.
My mother, she's half Choctaw, comes from Violet Springs, Oklahoma.
Four bars, a bank, and a big old cemetery,
It used to be called Violet Springs,
Before Oklahoma territory and the Indian territories joined.
Then they called the town Conoway, Strings of Pearls.
My momma, she's a member of the Junior Service League,
The Daughters of the American Revolution,
And the Shawnee Mother's Club.
Hell, there used to be oil all over the place.
My people used to bathe in it.
Came from Bugtussel, Buckchital, Watishomingo, and Skullyville.
I got a cousin, Robert Kee, that's a big Chickasaw name you know.
Old Robert is a pretty big lawyer nowadays, he's won a few cases.
But he goes to sleep sometimes at trials.
I asked him one time, how come he goes to sleep so much.
Hell, he says, it doesn't matter what that lyin' bastard says.
Our witnesses can lie as good as his, unless, of course,
He's payin' 'em more than we're payin' ours.'"
"Well, can you speak any Choctaw?" Drum asks him.
"Damn right," he says.
"The words that have come down to me from my grandfather are,
'Skully pu-to-me ... give me the money,'
And 'ish kish ba-lu-fu ... kiss my ass.'
The word for 'pussy' was lost somewhere
Near here, along the Trail of Tears."

To the North, Arizona

The Anasazi and the Park Ranger
(Keet Seel Indian Ruins, Where the Anasazi
People Lived Seven Hundred Years Ago)

Gave an old hitchhiking Indian,
Maybe ninety years old, a ride on Highway 89.
He waves his hand in front of his face.
"Hot," he says, drinks three glasses of water.
The kids make sandwiches, pass 'em up to
Him from the back of the camper.
He knows just a few words of English, but after another day,
Drum sees why he hasn't bothered to learn it.
They pass some horses. "Horse," says Drum. "Horse," he says, *"Klee."*
"Shee," Drum says. He points to the side of his mouth,
Pulls an edge back, *"Klee."* He shows Drum how to say it.
They talk with sign language. He points ... *"Betatakin* ... hill."
He makes a swoop over and down with his hand
Showin' where they need to go.
They drop him off by a crossroads, shinin' old eyes.
He opens the truck door, gets out, turns around.
Bows, nods, "Thank you, thank you," laughin',
Light as the wind in these driftin' sands.
His turquoise belt and beads all a-jinglin'
Goes along on his way.

They go on their way
Sunlight just setting on Tsegi town.
Twilight running on the cliffs in the canyons ...
They drive on into the park campground,
Wake about five in the morning.
Drum gets up the three kids and wife.
They eat breakfast and head on over to park headquarters.
"You're five people," the ranger says,
"We have four permits to go to Keet Seel ruins today.
It's sixteen miles round-trip.
Go on down, if you meet a nice ranger,

He'll probably let you all go in."
Sandstone cliffs carved by the cutting creek waters,
Swallows whistling, Twheee, twheee, twheee,
Twheee, twheee, twheee, twheee, twheee.
They go following the creek up Keet Seel Canyon.
After eight miles, a thousand feet down
And ninety-six creek crossings
And lots of heat in the sandy canyons, they get there.
The park ranger is waiting for them. It's a woman.
"What, you have only one canteen for a family of five?" she says.
"That's dangerous! You can't drink that water, it's polluted.
There are horses and cows grazing here."
Three cows and five horses, tracks of two more cows coming
On the trail, in eight miles of open country.
Drum thinks to himself, "Cows have been drinking
The people's piss in the rivers for centuries,
Do you think a little cow-piss will kill you?"
"I can only take four in your party," she says.
She must have known what Drum was thinking.
Drum's wife and the kids climb the ladder up into the ruins.
Drum sits down happily to write this poem.
"Ah, rippling creeks running here in the sunlight
Fed by springs and seeps.
Governments and parks and administrators,
Doling out water and feed and care.
Robots on schedules and automatons.
Anasazi people, you're lucky you're done and gone.
I'll just stay here drinking this old cow-piss water,
A little bit longer,
And come drift here with your spirits
In a few more years."

Indians

The frail form of El Apache,
The blue blood vessels in his neck,
His cracked lips saying,
"Then, horseback, I began to follow
The trail of my people.
'The Old Ones.'
They said, 'Do not listen to the wind.
It might call your name.
Then you will die.'"

. . . . .

TURQUOISE STONES IN THE CREEK BED ...

THE SOUND OF THE HORSE'S HOOVES IN THE SAND.

DRUG CULTURE
ON THE BORDERLINE

Hear the cutting sound in the air ...
A sound heard only once before,
On the grey ledge of a cliff,
When the wings of a passing eagle
Were set to strike,
And the eagle dove towards its prey.
In that moment out of time,
Before the curved talons
Hit the soft flesh and carved into bone,
The knowing jackrabbit heard
The last ripping sound
Of the wind in the eagle's feathers.

I. *El Tigre*

Cesario Alonso comes into the bar,
Stops a moment in the doorway, looks around the room.
He comes to sit at the table.
Talon hands, gentle, sets a glass so quietly down,
There is no sound, no tip of the glass.
But a possibility of another touch,
A smooth movement, that can end quick as a heartbeat,
In the buckhorn cradle of his rifle sight.
When he looks into another man's eyes,
He holds the eyes as long as he wishes, then he lets them go.
Those black pupils have seen all they need to see, to know.
Yo soy medio Apache, I am half Apache.
Yokiwi was the father of my mother.
Her mother was White Mountain Apache.
Serrano was her name. It is the word for the frozen dew
That shines at daybreak in the morning light.

We are the coyote who is born knowing
More about our prey than you will ever know.
We are the curved beak that pecks upon another's wing,
The vulture's beak that strips the flesh from the cow's tongue,
The cat's clawed foot that moves along the branches,
To where the small birds sit.
We are this borderline between death and life.

Our mothers, our fathers, were Indian and part Indian,
But we are no more animals than yourself,
Though all of us, I think, are animal.
It is only that you follow sounds of words
In this Gadsden Hotel bar. You hunt them.
It is the same to us as the killing of a deer.
To us, the drugs are food and clothes,
And allow our families to live.
The sound of the Borderland waters
That flow in your canyon,
Sound as though a wind were coming
Through cedar limbs by the sides of the cliffs.

Our women and children were formed
Of those same winds and waters.
For generations, they have passed like the wind,
Like water, through strands of barbwire,
The spines of mountains, to smuggle the cattle,
The *mescal*, the drugs, whatever has been,
Or is, worth more across the other side of that borderline
The strands of barbwire are no more to us than a few thorns
On a mesquite limb, across a mountain,
Or arroyo, or a canyon on our way.
You, yourself, know the ease, because you have passed
Across the thorns of this Borderland.

Many of us, the judges have sent to prison.
But to be imprisoned concentrates the limits of our desires,
Who we have been, and who we will be,
After looking from between the bars.
When first we come,
We do not know we will be anyone different
Than who we were before we went within the bars.
As though we had only known one hand
That played upon the keys of a piano,
When we were outside of the bars
And another hand played the darkness
We would become, when we were within.

But faith and belief are what bring our children into being,
Belief, as the tune upon the keys, when one is released from prison,
And the bars of the music break open to the sky and earth,
And a creeping of the light, as day and night meet, touch, blend,
To make the wind begin to move the limbs and oak branches.

We go through the land
As animals of *la madrugada,* the halflight.
When the light and the darkness come together,
We feel dusklight as though it were a deepening cut in our skin.
At dusk, something in us begins to want.
One can see this, watching a caged lion,
When nothing is before him but bars.

The lion feels the changing light in his body.
His head, his spine, lower, and the vertical, biting slits
Of his eyes begin to cast from side to side.

II. The Tracked Makes the Tracker

The ones I hire to carry the drugs are fine trackers,
So they, themselves, know how to leave few tracks.
One especially, when he sees signs,
His body will begin to curve
Into the shape of the animal he can still see,
Running across the land,
Though the body of the animal is long since gone.
"*Mira*, look," he once said,
As his body assumed the curve
And his feet assumed the position
Of a lion's running paws.
"*Así pintó la huella*,
In this way he made the track."

III. How We Feel

To a deer, the lion is evil incarnate,
To the lion, the deer is simply dinner.
Drum heard Don Cesario and knew he spoke a truth.
"Of what value is truth
If one cannot give it to another?"
Each had given his hand, and in that handshake agreed
That there would be no more passage of the drugs
Endangering the ranch.
"I would not smuggle the drugs," says the ranch hand.
"I would cut my throat before I smuggled."
The drugs' worth had no equal in a *vaquero's* life,
So he bought them to sell them,
Through the barbwire of the borderline.

Truth will not begin to clothe our women,
Nor put food in our children's mouths.
All of us lie, we who occupy the borderline
Between darkness and light,
We, who are like the Earth itself,
Who knows that the end of the day
Is the beginning of the borders of the night.

"*El tata Dios era chueco, era el mero chingón.*
Grandfather God was crooked,
He was the true mother#%*er.
Por eso nosotros salimos chuecos.
For that reason we come out crooked."

IV. To Lie Well

To lie well is sometimes a sadness.
To steal and to lie well,
A lie must be given to another with joy,
The same joy in recognizing the daily warmth
Of the dawnlight when it comes over the mountains.

In this way, it is easy to pass the drugs before your eyes.
We are as the smoke of your chimney fire that warms you.
You see us in the halflight only for a moment,
Then we disappear. You see only grasses,
The mesquite limbs, and the blueness coming into the sky.

But the rich rancher today is not like us.
He has forgotten what gave him his power.
You must remember the difference
Between us and him is that now, he has money.
He does not want us to smuggle the drugs across his land,

As his father smuggled the *mescal* and
Rustled cattle from his American neighbor,
Taking the carcass to town under a tarp
In the back of his pickup truck.
The rich rancher today has not earned money in our way.
He has not killed, nor has he lied.
His ranch was given to him by the chance of his mother's birth,
As all birth is a hand, whose opening palm
Lets the dice fall onto the table where they will.
The rich rancher today does not know this.
He thinks that right action should be rewarded, that there is truth.

We think to ourselves, we will teach him who God is.
We will show him the rock-cut ribs of the Earth,
The blood red arroyos that flow from them.
If he interferes with us when we cross the drugs,
His woman, his children, may be painted in blood.
Before we were *vaqueros*, we hunted and tracked.

V. Centuries of Patience

For centuries we have known time with a patience
Your people have forgotten.
To know where you will go and what you will do,
We simply watch.
When one pair of eyes leaves your face,
Another will take its place.
Night and day, we know where you are.
The *vaqueros* have done with your ranch
What you yourself would have done,
Had you agreed with a cousin or brother,
To place the drugs on the North side of the canyon.
You must know it is necessary
That someone smuggle the drugs.
The gringos require them and pay well.
We say, do not let *estranjeros*, the strangers, come here
To our land to smuggle the drugs.
Let us keep this *negocio* among ourselves.

If we were to pass the drugs before you tomorrow,
You would see nothing.
You would see your ranch pickup truck,
With the youngest of your *vaqueros* going to the boneyard.
The older men would be near to help
With whatever needed to be done.
If you asked him, the boy would say
He was going to the boneyard, to look for a rod
To repair the tailgate lever of your tan pickup truck.
He would check on the drugs.
My people, called *burros*, would come in the night,
Preferably, just before a rain,
or when the rain was falling.
In the morning, there would not be even a track.
We would talk about what we were doing in front of you,
In a knowing language,
And you would not know what we were saying.

VI. Horse Breakers

Always we have been horse breakers,
But we apply what we have learned,
In the breaking of the horses, to you.
The first thing a *vaquero* does when breaking a colt
Is to immobilize him by placing hobbles
Just above his hooves, to give him fear.
Then, to take away the fear, we sack him out.
We slap him with a gunnysack, all over his body.
He becomes used to this slapping, touching,
Even to his most private parts.
This is so that later, a saddle may be thrown onto his back.
This we do to you.
When we are going to move the drugs,
We race our truck engines. We race from your big tan shed
To your pineboard barn. Then we drive back again.
Then we go to your boneyard.
Then we carry a little hay to feed your horses.

But just when you think we are going to leave
For the borderline, and the Escondida Canyon,
To bring the drugs, we come back to your house,
To carry your trash to the dump.
When you no longer pay attention to anything we do,
We have, so to speak, sacked you out.
Then, we put the saddle of the drugs on your back.
We step upon you and ride you in the same way
We would ride a colt. We move the drugs past you
Without your knowing. We befriend your dog,
We ride your horses, we ride the movement of your cows,
We ride your life and your woman's life.
Quicker than you can ever think, this sand
Where your house is built can be washed away.
And though I tell you this now, you are like a colt,
Powerless to change one flick of our reins
Upon your neck.

The drugs will go to Douglas, to be handed
To a sharkskin jacket, a blue-black vest, filled
With one hundred solid crosses of silver,
A golden chain around a brown neck.
The drugs will float in glued tubes of plastic pipe,
In the gas tank of the yellow, 1978 short-bed Chevy pickup.

VII. Betrayal

A man always knows who his enemies are.
It is his friends he must watch.
I had an American *amigo*. When he had trouble,
He flicked his rifle lever and a cartridge went into the action.
He would say, "Don't fuck with me, man, I'll blow you away."
He had very little trouble.
But he needed to betray,
Like another man might need to do a job well,
To work at what he knew and had always done.
The man was good at his job.
I knew him for years, but I never knew what was hidden
Within him, that wanted to speak out,
As each day, his betrayal spoke.
At first, I noticed it as small lies.
He is no longer with us.

VIII. The Mules

Another of my mules was a thief,
Occupying the position of a foreman on a large ranch.
The position was very difficult,
For he was put in charge of the rich rancher's belongings.
As a man, he felt obligated to protect those goods.
He was proud.
He determined that if he were put in charge,
He would do that job.
But he was still a thief.
Everything inside of him told him he was a thief.
When he went to the rich rancher's boneyard,
He thought, "What is there left here,
That can still be of use to me?"
When he found an iron bar,
Or used a Stillson wrench, he took it.
He took a horseshoeing anvil.
Another man, who worked for me
Until he became too old, was Don Matías.

When a man can no longer see the front sight
Of his pistol in the firelight, then he is of little use to me,
Because one cannot trust that the trigger will be pulled
At the correct moment.

IX. The Picture

Sometimes, when you stay at Gray Ranch in the Animas Valley,
You will recall your old friend, José,
Who you had not seen in twenty years.
We sent him to pay you a visit.
We needed a picture of you and where you live.
If someday you are to give us trouble, we will set you up,
By leaving drugs at the place where you stay.
The Law will come for you and for your son.
Already, we have left drugs at this ranch.
We will make sure the arrest is in the newspapers,
In Las Cruces, Albuquerque, and El Paso.
If you continue to create difficulties,
Both you and I know ways to deal with outlaw horses.
One man was very insistent.
He continued to give trouble to my friends.
It was in the vicinity of Antelope Wells.
They cut out his tongue. They cut off his balls.
They dropped him from a helicopter onto the road.

X. The Horror

We do the same things on the inside
That we do on the outside.
We lie, we cheat, we steal.
But in 1980, in Albuquerque,
We put a man's whole body
Through the prison bone grinder.
We began with his hands.
He never stopped screaming.

• • • • •

TURQUOISE STONES IN THE CREEK BED ...
        THE SOUND OF THE HORSE'S HOOVES IN THE SAND.

OUR LANDS
IN THE BELLY OF THE BEAST

To give heart in the four directions ...
What still lies by the rivers and the mountains ...
What has disappeared into towns and highways ...
Old cowboys riding,
Their broad-brimmed hats pulled down low
Over their eyes, so they don't have to see
What their country has become.

TO THE EAST

Our Lands in the Belly of the Beast

Businessmen Overheard in the Palm Court Restaurant, Plaza Hotel, New York City, America

Take them, invite them out to lunch, don't get attached.
It's money, it's property, it's real estate, it's things, you say.
Do you want to sell?
What do you want to pay me to sell it for you?
We made fifty or sixty million. He died penniless.
His children asked us for one thousand dollars for the funeral.
It was tax deductible. Of course, we gave it to them.
Is it legal? The government pays lip service,
But the competition is fierce. You will have no license.
You will be seen as a mortgage consultant, a foreigner,
Your English will not be like theirs.
The property will be worth more
Than eight to ten times what we pay for it.
You will ask them for three or four,
But before they know it, you will get ten million.
When I am going to foreclose,
I pay the lawyers, maybe fifty thousand,
Four percent, three percent, five percent.
The poor man never wants to pay the lawyers,
So you know the poor man will lose.
These companies are like candy stores.
Make all the dough you can. Buy today, sell 'em short.
Take them; invite them out to lunch.
Subdivisions in mountain valleys,
Wild running rivers, country ways of livelihood,
Deer, cowboys, mountain lions, javelina,
Don't get attached. It's money. It's property.
It's real estate. It's things.
Take them; invite them out to lunch.

The Center of the World

Wall Street is the New World's Lovers' Lane

There are company profiles, computer dating,
Courtships, seductions, broken engagements,
Disillusionments, aborted deals, bastards, offspring.
There are trousseaus, gambling for dowries, innuendo,
Prostitution, merger specialists, marriage brokers,
Priests, affairs, and adultery.
There are white knights, Prince Charmings,
To chaperone a company's virgin body.
Wined, dined, those first times in a soft bed
With clean sheets, the Oak Bar at the Plaza Hotel,
Honeymoon suites, the Downtown Association.
Companies are just like women: each one wants to believe.
Futures, corporate marriages, physical and psychological securities.
Merger prospectus, true love, guile and persuasion.
This is the way we convince them that it's real.
It's all illusion.
It's wine, dine, flatter, corporate jets to love and protect.
It's payouts, takeovers, one company set up to be raped by another.
They sleep with you when they don't want to.
One corporation does another's bidding.
Heads of state wed money market bonds together,
Politicians and lawyers embrace at the United Nations.
Tables turn, the seduced company ends up in control.
Will they still be together seven years from now?
Common law.
More than half the mergers don't work out,
About the current divorce rate.
What are the corporate executives really willing to give up?
Reputations, honor, integrity, friendship.
There is wheeling and dealing, all or nothing at all,
Hardball, the jugular instinct. What is he really after?
The keys to chastity. Disruptions, slaves, dirty laundry,
Indecent exposure, it's all shining in their eyes.
Gold and silver, laser beams, satellites.
The New York Stock Exchange, The Federal Reserve,

The J.P. Morgan Guarantee Bank and the Trinity Church.
Soap-boxers hollering about the Truth and Hope and Charity,
Our lands all gone away in a moment's dream.

—Voice of WEB TURNER

A Businessman Overheard

Each One Wants to Believe

He is seedy. He is disingenuous.
He is leisure-suited East Coast sleaze.
He wears his ruby digital watch.
His voice comes from the table for two.
"Hey baby, you're the one.
You know, I would say this only to you.
You've got the jugular instinct.
I like you."

—Voice of BILL DURHAM

The Light

A Cab Driver

"I been robbed eight times," the black cab driver says.
"The cops, they tells us, 'When that guy aims his gun at you
And his finger begins to shake,
That's when you know he's goin' to pull the trigger.'
That hijacker, he says, 'Give me your money.'
And I gave him sixty-seven bucks,
But he thought I had more and he told me, 'Git out of the cab.'
He told me, 'Turn around,' and I said, 'Buddy, if you goin' to kill me,
You goin' to kill me with me lookin' you in the eyes.'
The bullet it hit me in the neck. It knocked me back over into the ditch.
I jumped about two feet high, I couldn't help it.
Finally after awhile, I crawled back onto the highway
And two old white ladies stopped for me and took me to the hospital.
That hijacker, I could feel something wrong about him
As soon as he got into the cab.
The cops, they tells us cabbies things. They say, 'Turn on the light,'
When I turned on the light that hijacker he got all nervous
He said he ain't a-gonna go ridin' down the street with no light a-shinin.'
That light is so a man can see. I shoulda left that shining light on."

The Race

Those Mafia guys, they walk you down a dark alley
So you can't tell who they are, or how many of 'em there are.
They say, "We want your horse to lose."
I say, "I can't hold up that horse, if you hold him up he runs faster."
They say, "Then give him his head. Sometimes jockeys just disappear."
I was head of the association. I had a family. My wife, a boy and a girl.
What else could I do?

TO THE WEST

Government

A Rancher's Tale

A voice comes from Ben's table,
In the Southeast corner of the barroom.
"The government's got a lotta information.
I dunno whether it's true or not,
But they typed it up and they put it in a book.
You know, they're just like chickens peckin'.
You throw some mixed grain onto the ground,
And the biggest ones begin pickin' up the best grain.
Then the others take their turn,
Till pretty soon all that grain's gone.
That's politics and politicians and the way
The government throws money away,
Here, on this borderline.
I used to watch the members of Congress.
They do this kind of Mandarin bow from the waist.
It kinda looks like an oil rig a-workin'.
The whole system would come unglued
If anybody really began to question it.
In politics, the winner is the one who can fake
Sincerity and still get done what he wants.
Government departments and agencies are
A lotta people doin' somethin' on paper,
And on that paper, what they're doin' looks real good,
But off of that paper, what they're doin's
More and more of nothin'.
For instance, there's a few cases of scabies
Discovered in the state.
The U.S. Department of Agriculture
Has money allotted to it each year,
Just like the Forest Service and all of
The governmental agencies and departments.
If that money isn't spent,
They won't get as much money the next year.

'OK, we're gonna mobilize a big plan,' they say.
On paper it looks real good.
Hire temporary people whose salaries don't
Show up when President Carter says he's reduced
The number of employees in the government departments.
The more people in the government department,
The more important the head of that department is.
The more money he makes and the more reason there is
For him bein' there.
In reality, there're already too many men in that department.
If scabies breaks out, somebody's goin' to see it,
A rancher, a farmer, a cattle inspector,
Somebody at a livestock auction.
You don't need all of them tea-sippin' fag supervisors,
Heads of government department who start a-shakin'
If they don't see neon.
Goddamn government people,
May be pretty good human beings one on one,
But they *ain't for shit* in comin'
In contact with ranchers and farmers.
Ranchers and farmers don't want them nitpickin' programs
That are supposed to be helpin' them.
Government people don't realize that some poor SOB
Like you and me was sufferin', tryin' to make a livin'
Out there in them canyons, right on that spot,
Where they want to put
A Coronado Forest Service Visitors' Center.
Government employees don't have enough to do.
The name of the game in government is,
'Don't make any decision you can be held responsible for.'
It isn't good to have common sense.
That whole dang system corrupts people.
Once the USDA provided millions of taxpayers' dollars
To eradicate the nonexistent hoof-and-mouth disease
In Mexico. If that eradication program had continued any longer,
It might of destroyed the entire economy of Mexico.
Usin' their Sanitary Rifle program, they killed

More'n a million and four hundred thousand head
Of cloven-hooved animals,
During 1946 and '47.
They got a lot of information,
But I don't know whether it is true or not, they typed it up."

—*Voice of* BILL BRYAN

Getting the Job Done

Another Rancher's Tale

Another rancher at Ben's table begins telling
About the Bureau of Land Management.
"A young man comes to the door of our house in town.
Him and his agency manage the Bureau of Land Management
On our ranch.
My cowboy's driven him forty miles to town for help.
'I'm from that group of eight vehicles that didn't quite make it.
Up Guadalupe Canyon,' he says.
'We stayed a couple of days.
We placed some mistnets to catch bats.
I think they must of washed away 'cause I can't find 'em.
Mine was the last vehicle to leave.
I stayed lookin' at plants and birds.
It was a real nice day, and I just drove right into
That creek without lookin'.
That truck had four-wheel drive,
But the tires must of hit a soft spot.
There was so little water, I didn't imagine
I might be in trouble. I guess I should of known.
The truck stalled in the middle of that creek.
I set for two or three minutes tryin' to start the engine.
Where I was, it hadn't hardly rained, but I think
There must of been rain somewhere up the canyon.
When I looked out of the window of that truck,

The water was gradually risin' up the side of the door.
I stayed, tryin' to start that truck till the whole truck body
Started rockin' and then floatin'.
Then the water started comin' in through the window.
I rolled down the downstream window
And climbed out onto the hood.
The truck was rockin' like all get-out.
I jumped for shore but didn't quite make it.
I thought maybe I'd better walk back to my camp,
To try and pull myself together.
When I got back to camp I saw that a great big limb
From a sycamore tree'd fallen right on top of my tent,
And smashed it like a pretzel.
I hate to think what would of happened
If I'd been in that tent.
I went to bed and woke this morning and hoped
It all had been a bad dream ...
But no such luck.
I hate to think what would of happened if I'd of been in that tent.
I dunno, I think maybe somebody's tryin' to tell me something.
I lay there in my sleeping bag,
Thinkin' of the birds and the beautiful canyon,
'Cause I hated to think of that government truck,
With the creek flowin' over the hood.
I got up and walked to the truck to get the canteen,
Where it was hangin' on the pickup bed,
'Cause I thought I might need some drinkin' water.
I guess I really went back to see if that truck was still there.
I was surprised to see it.
I waded to the truck and crawled into a window
To try the starter.
The engine barely turned. I thought it was best
To leave it while the battery still had some juice.
I'd been readin' a copy of Ernest Hemingway's
Islands in the Stream.
Left it on the dashboard. The last I saw,

It was floatin' down the creek. I had a refrigerator-freezer
That plugged into the cigarette lighter.
It hadn't floated out of the window yet.
The frame's restin' on the sand in the creek bed.
All the wheels're covered with sand.
You can just see a little bit of one front wheel,
And the creek water flowed over the engine all night.
What do we do?' the BLM guy asked me.
'Well,' I said, 'I reckon I could bring my bulldozer
Three miles up the canyon and pull you out.'
'I dunno about that,' he says.
'I'll have to call Government Services Agency who leased
The trucks to the BLM,
To see what their correct procedure is in a case like this.
We don't want to get it out in a way
That they won't authorize.'
So he made the call.
The office said to tow that truck two hundred and fifty miles
To Las Cruces, but he didn't have no money to rent a tow bar.
I took him to the tow bar rental garage,
And offered to loan him the sixty-seven dollars for that tow bar.
He called the Bureau of Land Management in Las Cruces,
To see if they'd pay back the loan.
'They probably will,' a nice girl said,
'But it may take an awful long time for the paperwork to be processed.'
After a day or two, he left the ranch and Douglas,
Being towed behind another government truck that'd been sent to save him.
He thanked me for my help, and for my cowboy bringin' him into town,
And for the meals my wife gave him, and the use of my bulldozer,
And the telephone, and the loan of sixty-seven dollars.
I thanked him for his help in managin' my ranch."
"Yep," says Bill Bryan, "with a little help
The government sure gets the job done."

The Sale of Beauty in the Desert

At the Restaurant Called Mélange, Tucson, Arizona, 1986

Potted plants along an oak ledge separate the tables,
Only green philodendron leaves, ornamental palms
To screen the two men who talk to one another.
"He's trying to suck you in, scam you," the old man says.
"Don't give him a penny. He says he's got Vincent in his pocket.
He says if he doesn't have Vincent, he's gonna bury Vincent.
You know you got no fuckin' sewer lines, you got nothin'.
All the mistakes that were made here in this city,
They can be made here again in the country.
I bought land for ten cents a foot.
In a year I sold the land for twenty dollars a foot.
But if you got no fuckin' sewer lines, you got nothin'.
The key is to control the zoning.
We pay whatever it takes to keep control of zoning.
One man was hard to convince. I had to kill him," the old man says.
"Then I went to his funeral in Florida.
His son jumps up in front of five hundred people.
'You killed my father,' he says.
A half million for you," the old man says. "A million for me ..."
Southwest wind blowing across the light threads of palo verde leaves.
Rock rip-rapped walls, cement faces.
One killdeer who still calls here across the arroyo sands—
"But you got no fuckin' sewer lines, you got nothin—"
A killdeer calling, "Till Deo, Till Deo."
In Sancto Deo, In Holy God, Till Deo, Till Deo, Till Deo ...

They Told Me Thirty-five Years Ago ...

Politics and the Weather

"The only trouble talkin' with old-timers
About politics and the weather,"
Says Ben Williams, eighty-two come next March,
"Is to prove 'em wrong, you've got to outlive 'em.
Now there's been a hell of a lot of 'em I've proved wrong,
But a man gets no satisfaction from it,
Because by that time it's too late to argue.
If you could just dig 'em up for about ten minutes.
The new generation won't believe
Anythin' you tell 'em, and it's too late
To argue with the old generation.

Everybody's got a crystal ball.
None of 'em are worth a damn."

TO THE NORTH

Anthropology

Gathering Cattle for the Fish Creek Cattle Association before the Snows Trap 'Em in the High Country

A few snowflakes falling,
Light clean smell of the wind in the sage.
"It takes these cold nights to make a good day,"
Says Lester Jacobsen, Melody Ranch foreman.
Melting frost on the wheat grasses,
Turning to dewdrops in that first morning light.
"We had a pretty hard, cold Winter last year," Lester says.
"There's sure gonna be lots of new babies, come this Fall."
Cattle drifting ahead of our horses' hooves,
Drifting down the trails past Slate Creek, Crystal Creek.
Brown backs of Hereford cows,
Snowy clouds on the mountain peaks,
Crystal Flats to Horsetail, along the Gros Ventre River trail.

Quick, ride across the river,
Through those falling yellow aspen leaves,
Cows and calves are slipping away.
Steamy mists drifting off the warm springs we pass,
Drifting off over the scattered snows.
A longhorn bull jumps over the fence onto the highway past Kelly,
Starts all the bulls to fighting,
Scatters cows and calves all over the slick highway,
Big semi trucks waiting to pass.
"We'll pick 'em up tomorrow.
Leave 'em over there," says Lester,
"By that cottonwood tree, just past the Mormon Road,
Where the buck rail fence runs in from the West.
When those cold snows get to flyin',
These old cows come a-trailin' down the high country,
Through these mountain passes.
They've done it before, they've learned the way.
Yep," says Lester, "they come a-trailin' down here,
One followin' after the other,
Just as smooth as a school marm's leg."

—*Voice of* LESTER JACOBSEN

The Salmon

Sliding, gliding, writhing over the rounded rocks of this last river,
Skin and fins battered from the long sea swells and wind-torn waves,
They come here, grey and silver, flashing,
Through the fingers of the cliffs,
Salt ebb and flow of those tidal waters.
Each fish to follow the clear water, mixed with the scent of earth,
To come home at last from that open sea,
To those first spawning sands,
Where he and she were born.
Two flashes of silver, swimming down the birth stream,
To grow in that sea we know, then changed, come back,
Old, mottled, spawned-out flesh to die.
Waking on the edge of that river, I watch them pass me by,
Below blue glacier mountains and cliffs.
Here the fingers of that first morning light
Reach through the low mists,
To touch the swollen belly of swirling spawning sands.
Those grey shapes in the waves and waters,
That carve a lifeline into the palms of our hands,
Beyond a last, ringed, pool of light and swirling sky.
I can hear them call to me from that far river,
The spawning, wet womb where I was born.
An old salmon now, still strong and firm and silver, flashing, in his tides,
Swimming back towards those rings of light and dawn.
Now, in this sunlit mirror of the water,
In the long bend of this last stream,
I see those spawned-out spirits and mottled bodies float,
Float through these mists below the mountains,
Float in the ebb and flow of the tide pools,
Float with our hearts, drawn back to the sea.

Old Worlds Drifting Away, Santa Fe, New Mexico

"My god, in one half hour from when they push that button
The World, the Northern Hemisphere is gone,"
Says Stanislav Ulam, co-inventor of the hydrogen bomb,
"But I am old, maybe I won't see it. Memory, no one knows
What it is, whether it's electric current or carried by molecules.
First you forget names, then you forget faces, then you forget
To zip up your fly, then you forget to zip it down."
Ah, worlds and old men with sparkling grey eyes.
"Have a good trip," he says when we part.
Worlds in the desert country drifting away ...

TO THE SOUTH

A Trembling Wind

The Backbone of the Sierra Madre

Me and Blue Horse are prowling the country.
We top out on a high ridgeline.
I lift only the weight of the leather reins in my fingers.
That's all it takes, Blue Horse is glad to stop to rest.
A light wind from the South eases along that ridge top.
He perks his left ear, hearing the far sound of an engine.
We look off to the South into Old Mexico.
Two big, bobtail trucks move like red ants in the distances.
They crawl towards us, towards that place
Where there used to be a seep spring and a cottonwood tree,
Where the old trail used to come into the Puerta Colorada.
Now, there are bulldozed white rock slides.
They spill down the green mountain sides
To kill tall, stranded grasses left after the Summer rains.
In some empty pit in my chest, I feel the hollow ache.
Grey pavement through old mountain canyons and passes,
Road cuts where there were only trails and gramma grasses.

*Vaquero*s riding past soft adobe, lamp-lit houses.
Now the knife of this new highway called Mexico Route 2
Wounds the rock-rippled ranges of the high Sierra.
It slashes through the limbs of the stretching Animas Valley,
This new highway of jake brake roaring, diesel smoke choking loads.
The skeletons of turned-up truck bodies litter these mountain ranges
That red ants have ripped, blasted, bulldozed, and smashed.
Now, each fresh world of concrete, each new trophy housed high peak,
Slashes through the Earth's old arroyo runes singing in our blood.
Each new subdivision clots the nerves and the cracks in our backs.
Each new highway scars the fingers of our bloody hands,
The wrapped sinews of our bodies, the ancient seashell sands.
But at night, when a trembling wind from the South is just right,
We can hear those last voices of these mesas and arroyos calling.
They still echo through that cracked backbone of the high Sierra Madre.
They still echo through those canyons of the Cajón Bonito.
They still beat through our bloody hearts along Mexico Route 2.

BOOK FOUR

· · · · ·

Eternity

· · · · ·

· · · · ·

TURQUOISE STONES IN THE CREEK BED ...
       THE SOUND OF THE HORSE'S HOOVES IN THE SAND.

PREAMBLE

Here, hand in hand
Holding this moment together
Along a great rim of earth,
Holding together the world that we know,
Please bless us, mountains, mesas, arroyos,
And this deep Guadalupe Canyon bounty
We are about to eat.

Waiting

I.

To be the sound of the wind,
Blowing dust and old husks
Under the leaning walnut limbs.

II.

Waiting to be the sound of the stones,
As though they could own where you were born.
Coming out of some wet womb of the Earth,
Where the water flows down out of the mountains.

III.

Sunlight and clouds, this old canyon of Guadalupe.
Here, I've come to wait through the years for you.

IV.

To the sunlight, lighting green lichen rock ledges,
To the moonlight, on those same cliffs at evening,
To you and me, sitting beside them.
Sunlight and clouds, cliffs on the mountains,
All of us here a moment, then gone.

V.

Wildflowers opening, blooming in the Springtime,
Yellow and orange, blue in these mountain valleys ...
One cold night and all the bloom is gone.

VI.

So many hearts have gone before us,
Petals of old Spring flowers,
Wisps of cloud, crossing the wide blue sky.

Song of the Earth

Singings of the Earth, sing your songs into me,
Crack my head, break my bones,
Sing your songs at me.
Fire, teach me how to live like you burn,
Too much wood, and the flame goes out,
Too little wood, and we die away.
Yesterday is ashes, tomorrow's yet to come,
Only today does the flame burn bright.
White flowers, teach me how to listen in the Spring,
Stems breaking up through the rocks and the earth.
Blue skies, drop your blueness down into my eyes,
Come, and I'll hold you deep behind my eyes.
Arroyo waters, teach me how to run like you run,
Too much water, and your banks give way,
Too little water, and the stream runs dry.
Sunlight, teach me to live like you burn,
Too much light, and my heart gives way,
Too little light, and the flame is gone.
Setting suns, sing your shadows deep into my eyes,
Come, and I'll hold you there deep behind my eyes.
Mesquite tree limbs, sway your shadows softly on my life.
Come, and I'll hold you here deep inside my eyes.
Rippling creeks, sing your songs down into my ears.
Cut the earth, sing your stream beds
Deep into my whirling head.
Shining water, diamond water,
Cut your mirrors into my head.
Hide your mirrors behind my eyes,
So I won't know where I've been.
Hide your eyes behind my eyes,
So I won't know where I go.

LOVERS

"Would you do it all the same way again?" he asks.
"A man is a man, a woman is a woman,
And I was a woman," she said.

. . . . .

TURQUOISE STONES IN THE CREEK BED ...
THE SOUND OF THE HORSE'S HOOVES IN THE SAND.

Snow

The Beginning of this World

Ready to go, or to stay, there in that stillness,
I began to see before me
The rippled, long ridges and grey rims of the Sierra Madres.
Range upon range, fading into those desert valleys,
The blue distances at the far edge of Earth, of sky, and emptiness.
I remembered her long, dark hair.
I can feel her in my arms each time,
When the first Fall snow comes in the night to the desert country.
And then at dawn, when those grey points of pale light
Strike the white peaks and begin to come
Down the Western mountain slopes.
When each cedar limb and stem of the tall grasses
Bends to hold those rimmed shapes of the trembling whiteness,
As though the crystalline structure of the world
Were filled with living prisms of the rising sun's light,
That quiver and dance with each flake,
Till that glowing light falls around us,
Along the still, shadowed ground,
To begin to light again, the beginning of this world,
And bring the warmth of the day into our hands.

Who Are We Here, Wanting to Know?

Alma de Mi Alma
A Song of the *Vaqueros* of Mexico

> *El sauce y la palma, se mezclan con calma,*
> *Alma de mi alma, qué linda eres tú.*
> The willow and the palm,
> They gently touch each other.
> Alma of my soul, soul of my soul,
> How beautiful you were.

> Alma born 1953 to Don Crucito Alonzo,
> *Vaquero* in the Cañon de Dimas,
> Where the swallows come nesting,
> By the red cliffs in the Springtime Sonora, Mexico.

> Where do the swallows go, passing with the West wind?
> By the red cliffs they stay for a while, then go.
> When she was a young girl, her mother didn't want her,
> So took her to town to Doña Petra.

> Where do the swallows go, passing with these West winds?
> Where do they nest for a while and then go?
> When she was sweet sixteen, Doña Petra didn't want her,
> So she went to live with her uncle Peru.

> She was shot through the heart by Peru's jealous wife.
> She's buried in the *cañon* at El Ranchito.
> Where do your hates and your jealous loves go?
> Who are we here ... wanting to know?

> Who are we here, wanting to know?

Shy, whirling Alma, dancing your young-old eyes.
The carousing *vaqueros* chased all night,
Till the sunlight lit their camp on the town street,
Between our roundup *jefe*'s house and hers.

Como un águila, bajando a un lepe,
Roberto bailó con las señoritas in Agua Prieta
Like an eagle, dropping down on a dogie calf,
Roberto danced with the señoritas in Agua Prieta.

Where will the old Earth take you, dancing through the starlight?
Whirling you on and on, while she goes.
Where will the old Earth carry us, dancing through the starlight?
Whirling us all on and on while she goes.

Danced her through that old white house, where she lived.
One room, adobe mud, the other of cardboard and rusting pieces of rattling tin,
Where Petra served us *frijole* beans and *carne,*
As though we'd come driving steers along those dusty trails as kings.

Whirling you on and on while she goes,
Whirling us all on and on while she goes,
West from the San Bernardino River, through Galliardo Pass we rode
In the dusk light, lost two steers in the night-time.

Rode on again another day into Agua Prieta,
Through dirt streets and Mexican kids
Running by the sides of the road, throwing rocks at stray steers,
To keep them headed towards the border corrals.

Then with tequila and *corridos* floating through the cantinas,
And the women, and the songs, we forgot the dust, the wild cattle,
The cold of the mornings, the winding trails, and changed the town
To some whirling place, we didn't remember or know.

Where do those nights and the singing in your memories,
And the crossings of these valleys, and the sandy rivers go?
Where do those nights and the singing in our memories,
And the crossings of these lands, and the sandy rivers go?

And the *vaqueros*, who rode whistling
In those soft dark eyes,
While the swallows circled and drifted in the winds
Calling by the red cliffs in the Cañon de Dimas in Springtime.

Where will those loves, and your laughing black eyes,
And the winding river go?
Who are we here, wanting to know?
Who are we here, wanting to know?

—*Voice of* CARLOS YSLAVA

Alma de Mi Alma

Bury Them Deep

Then Leave No Witnesses

Josefina and Ramón were lovers.
She was head lady of the night in El Palacio in Naco.
He was El Burro, chief of police,
Macho, Yaqui Indian, ready to kill for money.
"*Pásele*, come in," she said, and offered a cup of coffee.
To the gringos, they are killers and thieves,
But that is how they stay alive.
"*Este burro me dió una patada en el ojo,*
This burro gave me a kick in the eye," she said.
A young girl's light walk still in her old legs,
Her left eye black and swollen.
So many lovers to build her home of adobe brick,
So many men between her feet in the soft light
Of the candle melting away.
El Burro laid his Colt .45 onto the coffee table.
They argued. She picked up his gun from the coffee table.
Quick as the hollow fang of a snake,
El Burro closed his hard hand upon her hand
He turned the muzzle of the Colt .45 to her head,
He squeezed her finger already on the trigger.
"She was only a woman of the night celebrating the New Year,"
He told the Law. "The gun went off too close to her head."
She's buried deep. There were no witnesses.

La Llorona

The Spanish legend of the weeping woman,
She who loved an *hidalgo*, a man of upper class.
She who drowned the two babes her man wanted.
She who wanders the arroyo sands hunting for them forever.
Now by those waters, her grey feathered soul is born a wailing night bird,
Whose heart was torn in a wind from the long branched centuries
That held Earth's steady nest wound with twigs,
Bits of down, threads of sunlit grass stems in the Springtime.
But when, one night in the twilight, she drowned her children and lost her man,
She didn't know how to go back to that woven home she came from.
So now when she moans among those pale shapes of arroyo shadows and piñons,
She wails for women and hunts babes who wander alone.
She who is Earth's tattered twin who wails for all who are lost,
Mothers, fathers, lovers, dead children, and stray dogs.
Who weeps for those old ghosts we have known
In the pale light and in the darkness.

For all of us forever to find our home in the dusk light each night.

A Marriage Blessing Song

Someday, when two lovers go to that place in their hearts,
They'll never know how to come to or go back to again,
Where those light fingers of their waving dreams
Have dreamt, with the blue sky and the wind and the sea,
Where the white clouds roll and hold you there,
And each night rolls and holds you there,
As though your eyes had looked into
The beginnings of the Earth and the wind and the sea.
Then, as though you two were winds that blew,
That touch and whirl by these desert peaks and creek waters,
As though, on your lips, soft winds came
And tangled their loves in your long arms and kissed,
Now, go on you two, across those waters,
Go on you two, across that sea.

• • • • •

Scraps of sisal rope
That were a hackamore,
Scraps of hide
That were a reata,
Scraps of you and me
Who were the life of lovers,
Gone into eternity.

Grand Canyon

A Man and a Woman

From this rimrock edge, two courting ravens
Dive, twist, fall outward,
Outward past white rock buttes,
Past scattered shards of mesas,
Shattered mountains beyond mountains,
The drop and fall of red cut ledge beyond ledge,
Sliding off towards the end of Earth.
Blue sky, white cloud, the wind, and emptiness,
Deep, deep down the rapids' sounds echo,
Rim to rimrock roaring flows, of the old river,
A wind beneath two ravens' wings.
A man and a woman stand together, watching,
Grains of sand, wandering towards the sea.
A trembling bridge to cross this emptiness,
Piñon trees and sunlight ...
You and me.

One Plum Tree Blossom

One Time I Knew

When there was just you and I
In some long-ago blooming,
That over the years, I'd forgotten,
In the light leaf shadows of you,
When I walk across the arroyo
From the tractor to the wheatfield.
White plum tree blossoms,
Come down here, come down away,
While the buds, like your dress of white flowers, fall,
The folds and the clearness of your petals darken.
That whiteness will be gone,
Before daylight drops here on the sandy earth.
Then you'll see.
White plum tree blossom,
Hurry down here, come down here
Out of your house, away ...
What will happen to you and me
When we've grown old, and thrown our seed
And we lie here in the sand,
Some old blossoms under a tree?
Ah, plum tree blossoms,
One time I knew ...
While the sun and rains come and go,
These Springtimes pass away ...
Come bloom here this Springtime
In the soft light sand with me.

THE RAINS

We Wait

With the fingers of my left hand,
I dig in the sand to follow the vanishing seep spring down.
Among the rocks and the lizards, I come to drink.
A bee moves over the rock beside me.
Grey-winged butterflies light on the willow tree.
Each day I follow the water table down through the sand,
Each day going a little bit deeper.
A curved bill thrasher and quail come to drink.
In this canyon reaching towards the dark holes in space,
We wait for the new water to well into our pool.

Hidden Waters

Then one day, your horse's hooves
Will carry you down around that bend,
In the curves of the shifting arroyo sands,
Where what you have waited for, for a lifetime,
Will suddenly be there before you,
To be seen and not seen only once or twice,
In those flows of a lifetime,
Every few hundred years.
There, what you have waited for,
Will appear in the shape of a *tinaja*,
A beautiful clear pool,
Where the mixing arroyo sands and the waters
Have cut the deep pool downward,
Ever deeper and deeper,
Into the flows of the waiting rock.
It is there, that you will drink
In those waters that wait before you.
So now, deer, mountain lions, coatimundis, javelina,
Come drink here, by the shy lips of this pool
Lips touching lips, you and I.

The First Summer Rains

I am the soft wind blowing in through the open window.
I am the sound of the chickens pecking,
Peeping around the bottom of the screen door.
I am the old hen cluck, cluck, cluck, cluck,
Worrying about where the young chicks are going.
I am the rooster crowing at four o'clock in the morning.
I am the drops of water dripping off the tin roof to the honeysuckle leaves.
A white-winged dove watching from the cottonwood tree
Calling to another dove way off across the canyon.
I am the sounds of the children playing,
Doing the evening chores down by the corrals.
Says Sadie, "No, no, Sethie, don't throw me into the water trough."
I am the mourning doves strutting their tails,
Walking along the length of a swaying limb, waiting to fly away.
I am the momma doves heavy with eggs,
Planing along to some nest through the air.
I am old friends, gone, remembered.
I am the rough flow of a horse's shod hooves
Running down some trail to nowhere.
I am what the new world throws away,
What the wind blows into the gulleys,
That blows into the fences on the edges of the towns
That sticks in the brush and the tumbleweeds and the leaves.
I am this day when the first Summer rains
Have come after all these months of dryness.
Arroyos, rippling, grasses growing, birds ...
All the cow country singing a different song.
I am all that stayed waiting ... after all that you wanted was gone.

Drifting

Cochise County

"When I came here to Douglas,
  Thirty-five years ago," Bill Bryan says,
"They told me it was a-goin' to rain.
  But I'm still here a-waitin'."
"Well, stick around," says Old Man Ben Williams,
  Lookin' into those blue distances away off to the East.
"That's a pretty good lookin' cloud,
  Driftin' across the South edge of that little peak.
  It just might come."

—Voices of BILL BRYAN *and* OLD MAN BEN WILLIAMS

If It's Raining

  Says the Mexican rancher Alfonso Ruíz,
  "Cada lluvia es un chorro de pesos.
  Every rain is a stream of dollars.
  ¿Hijo do la chingada, por qué no llueve?
  Goddamn, why won't it rain?
  ¿Si hay un Dios como dicen, por qué no llueve?
  No para mí, para los pobres animales.
  If there's a God as they say, why won't it rain?
  Not for me, but for the poor animals."

Dewdrops

Catching It on the Run

In the Springtime, when you know a rain
Has fallen way off down the canyon,
You can ride out just at daybreak,
To catch those dewdrops and the morning, shining,
Before the sunlight hits them hard and burns them all away,
And burns your heart, drifting along through the days,
And all the hope in those shining worlds
Goes off into the light wind ...
Goes drifting and drifts away.

Watching in the Dawnlight

Before the Rains

There is something the black phoebe sees
In those shapes in the cave,
When the water drips along the low ledge,
And then drops down into the pool.
And who are you and I,
Waiting by that same ledge,
Still drawn to each ocotillo, each desert blossom,
Each one of us, a drop of water,
Who waits to fall into the pool.

Listening Here to Hear

New Mexico

Windmill wells and waterholes goin' dry,
Sure don't look too good for these cows.
Makes you think the rain's never goin' to come.
Nothin' but empty, blue sky.
Short nights so hot you can hardly sleep.
Way before daylight, saddle up a stout horse,
To ride out, prowling through the rangelands,
To get these cattle through one more droughty day.
The black gnats swarming around your head,
Gnawing your eyes and your ears.
Rope those cows that will die, bogged in black mud,
On those cracked edges of the drying-up waterholes.
Slashing horns, hooking at your horse,
Sucking sounds of their mud-caked legs,
While you drag 'em away from that stinking mud,
With the smell of death.
The dry sands blowing, waiting here for the rain,
Worn out with what whirling wind will come,
To bring Lady Luck to you.
Those falling drops, touching light on your skin,
The white-winged doves by the seep willows, calling in your ears,
Listening here, to hear the sound of the rain.

—Voice of WALTER RAMSEY

A New Wind

Emptiness

Nothing but empty blue sky.
Go gamble with the high rolling earth.
Haul those yearling cattle
To Sonny Shore's Willcox Livestock Auction.
Pale, rumbling twilight in Old Mexico has fooled you.
Only heat lightning, and you,
And the cattle, and the dry grasses, and no rain.
Droughty cowboys, still looking towards that empty skyline,
Listening to a blown range song,
Cowboy hearts in the dust have always known.
Waiting here for the rain.
Then one day, you feel a new wind come,
Blow cool on the sweat of your sun-baked neck.
Smell that wetness sweeping past the blue mountain ranges,
The lightning cracking. As old Walter Ramsey says,
"Dry times are always thatta way.
When you think what you've waited for never will come,
That's what it takes, to bring you the rain."

—Voice of WALTER RAMSEY

When God Wills

Old Mexico

"Las lluvias son todo lo que hay que ver.
  The rains are everything there is to see," says Everisto,
"Mire las nubecitas,
  Look at the little clouds far off,
  Away to the South, along the horizon."
  In the early afternoon, they're still coming,
  Heading North, traveling closer and closer.
"No hay que mirar las nubes para no asustar el agua,
  Now don't look at those clouds," says Everisto,
"If you look, you'll scare the water away."
  In the late afternoon, early evening,
  A light breeze blowing in from the Southeast,
  The clouds becoming darker and darker,
  Massing above the ranch headquarters.
  Then white streaks of lightning,
  Stretching from high mountains to the sky,
  Crack, crack the thunder calls, then Boom BOOM
"No me cuentes mentiras, Cielito Lindo,"
  Everisto calls back to the sky,
"Don't tell me lies and stories, Beautiful Sky.
Hecha la, Cielito Lindo, hecha la.
  Let the rains come, Beautiful Sky,
  Do it now, do it now."
"Cuando Dios quiera,
  When God wills," says Roberto,
"When God wills, the waters will come from the clear sky."
  Waiting here for the rain.

—Voices of ROBERTO ESPINOSA *and* EVERISTO WASICA

The Weather

A Woman

"*¿Qué húbole?*" say the *vaqueros*, "How's it going?"
They greet one another in the morning,
Then they begin to talk about the weather.
"*Demasiado helado, y huela chinga,*" they say in the Wintertime,
"Too goddamn cold," and they tighten the white fleece
Of their Levi jacket, if they have one, a little bit tighter around the neck,
And if they have a bandana, they tuck it into the holes,
Where the cold comes in between the bandana and the fleece.
Almost always, it is too cold, or it is too hot, or a little bit hot.
There are traces and tracks of clouds, or there are no clouds,
Or it was too hot or too cold the day before.
They look to the South, they look to the East, they look to the North,
They look to the West, to see what those winds will bring.
So the *vaqueros* track to foretell their woman, the Earth,
As though each one could know her,
And feel her touch in the hope of rain.

Hearts

Arizona

In the Summertime monsoon season,
When the first light clouds begin to come
Drifting along those low mountain ridgelines,
Across the stretch of the desert valleys,
Then each cow in the herd begins to look upward,
Towards where the waters come from.
Cows and calves begin to graze away
From dusty, beaten-out water holes,
The hoof-hammered springs, windmills, and pipeline waters.
Then cow trails begin to go
Towards old odors of seeps and cloud mists,
The half-hope of rains, half fallin' down from sky to earth,
And so do our eyes go.
We, the people of the Borderlands,
Who look upwards to watch the clouds coming,
Across canyons and valleys, the desert mountain ranges,
Droplets of hope for one more year.
But if the rains don't come heavy and strong,
The mists of them fall to the earth and are gone.
Your woman's heart, her aching tears,
Waiting here for the rain.

Clouds

As Though You and I Were the First Drops ...

In the Summertime when the rains don't come,
Forming off to the South in the clear blue morning sky,
In the Springtime, in Winter, in the Fall too,
Clouds and women, drifting grains of the blowing sands,
After you've hoped as long as you can,
All you can do is wait,
Till the next light wind brings her home to you.

After a Few Drops of Rain at Dawn

Fragments of Sunlight Climb the Ridgeline

Fragments of cliff clouds roll along,
The blue coming into the morning light,
A soft wind in the cottonwood leaves.
I've come here to meet you in these desert morning mists.
I've come here to meet you by that high pass in the mountains.
I've come here to meet you in the old gold in the canyon,
Way off, nearly up to that place
Called Left Hand Tank Creek arroyo.
I've come here to meet you in this desert morning light.

From the White Cowbones

The Call of the Desert Rangelands

Wash me now, you Summer rains.
For more than a year, I've lain here, waiting for you,
While the old sideoats grass stems have shattered, split,
Thrown their seed, and blown away,
While the wandering ants
Crawled past the white cowbones.
Now wash the caked dust
From my cracked lips and my skin.
Let those clouds come blow again.
Grey with the rain waters,
Whirling through blue mountain ranges,
Past the rock cradles, the canyon rims,
Till the muddy arroyos roar
Across the desert valley floors,
Till the grama grasses green up
On the brown burning peaks,
Till the young grass stems head out
From the bare bone cradles of these canyon hills.
Wash me along the rims of arroyo rocks.
Carry the dust, carry the sands,
Carry these words, my seeds,
Down these blue desert valleys, away.

Flash Floods

What Could Have Been

I remember my old friend Charlie saying,
"Before we know, we do what we have done."
Memory is filled like a dry arroyo,
When the first edge of the water comes.
The water carries the pieces of lost lives,
Feathers of birds, bits of bark, tiny leaves,
Broken stems, new sideoats seeds,
Held in the sound of that grey, gravelly mass,
Mixing, swirling, rippling,
Through the sand and rocks.
But if the rain-bearing clouds,
Mixed with the sunlight,
Mixed with the draw of the far sea-tides
And wind-forming storms, are not enough,
Then, at some bottomless place,
What could have been a river,
Disappears, into the sands.

—Voice of CHARLES OLSON

What You Wanted

But sometimes the rains come too late.
Everything that you wanted to grow has died,
And those light seeds that you sowed,
That went drifting from your hand
Onto the ground, the rocks, and the weeds,
Came to push up into the sunlight
And the wind burned, dried, and blew them away.
The old womb, where the atoms are splitting,
Where the particles are hurtling off
Into some tiny infinitesimal space, I am that fire.
As Roberto says, "Quicker than you can ever think,
This sand where your house is built will be washed away."
Sound of the thunder, sounds of the dry creeks
Running full with water.

Seeds

Where nothing else will grow in this desert country,
Weeds and yellow flowers will come blooming here in the Springtime.
Weeds and yellow flowers some year when the light rains come,
Covering whole valleys between these blue mountain ranges,
Covering the ground with rainbow colors for miles and miles
Those seeds will be here blooming ...
That's all you need to know.

• • • • •

TURQUOISE STONES IN THE CREEK BED ...
THE SOUND OF THE HORSE'S HOOVES IN THE SAND.

AN ECOLOGY

The lay of the land,
The way of the man.

To Hold Back the Water

A Walk Down the Canyon

Because of one rock, five cottonwoods have come up.
Because of three grass stems, a sycamore tree has grown.
Because of a rain, high in the mountains,
Two Cooper's hawks raise their family of one.
Because of you and me taking this walk,
All of us are true.
Earth and sky along this dirt road,
One white cloud, passing by.

Light, Come Play with Me

Light is a whirl of all there is
That has been, that is to come.
One rock on the ridge above the draw
Slides down into the stream.
I sit to watch that rock come down.
Light and rock turn into dreams.
Old rocks who fall, who have made my mind ...
Shadows and light and wind on these grasses.
Come play with me beside this stream.
You bring me a world ...
I'll bring you some dreams.

The Borderlands

What does not change/is the will to change

CHARLES OLSON

I.

The borderline of a lion's pad print
Pressing into the grains of arroyo sands.
The borderline of a lion's heart
Beating with the blood's beat as fast as it can.
Now who are we who follow those same heartbeats?
We, like the lion, like to eat the fresh meat.

II.

The Borderlands are where change occurs.
Where one is becoming another
And where one life is left and another is found.
Birds in the air come to fly around us.
They are how far each creature leans towards another,
Each fly, each plant, each ocotillo blossom.
They are along the border of each cloud that passes by
On its way to go towards today, tomorrow, yesterday,

The borderline of starlight,
Light bursting through billions of years.
While you and I sit here beside it waiting
For the Borderlands to enter our beings
For all those times we will become.

III.

By the edge of the arroyo bank
Where the first Springtime flowers grow,
By the edge of the river,
By the edge of the snows,
By the edge of you and me,
By the edge of all we could ever know,
By the edge of the countries,
By the edge of a continent,
By the edge of the window,
By the edges of the eyes you look through,
By the edge of your hand touching mine ...
By the edges of a wing waiting.

Sitting on the Gray Ranch Porch before Dawn

Swallows

The great empty valley of the stretching Animas Mountains,
The great Sierra Madre ranges lying to the South,
All before us in this beginning before the dawn.
The emptiness here before us, away to the West,
The edge of emptiness, moving from the mountains to the East,
Then swallows come chittering from the barn roof eaves,
Crossing and recrossing what we couldn't see was there.
The light in the dark emptiness, swallows whirling through the air.

Buzzards

I. The Waiting Earth

Look at them, there in the dawn.
They are still there on their roosting tree.
Red heads, red necks, black wind-whistling bodies
Waiting on that perch to soar up into the morning.
Then, their great grey wings
Appear as the open arms of the mountain ranges,
Stretching outward to hold the horizon of the waiting Earth.
You and I sit by them, waiting
To fly to the end of that dawnlight.

II. Waiting to Cross Empty Blue Sky

Now come you desert winds.
Come drift the light sands around my curving eyelids.
Then come you young buzzards,
Wing fingers come touching, tilting, lifting, gliding
Across those canyon eons changing in the changing air,
Then away, away, away again.

Winged fingers lifting from the cottonwood limbs,
Wind fingers rising, falling, soaring, gliding
Outward, outward, from this old buzzard's roosting tree.
Winged bodies whirl up into the light,
Then come back touching, sailing, circling, gliding,
New winged fingers just for you and me,
Then away, away, away again.

III. Only the Tips of Our Wings to Know Where We Will Go

Crossing and recrossing those ancient trails through the whirling air,
Then planing off alone along the ridge lines of the mountain ranges,
The sands of the rock rippling seas.
But our old wings are tattered now,
Fading feathers falling away
Across the valleys, those ancient playas.
There, I'll come to meet you.
It will be like yesterday,
When we two flew through all the worlds together.
Now, new wing feathers just for you and me,
Away away away

A Flight

Crossing the Canyons

One day I thought a leaf was a bird,
It flew so high.
It turned, it whirled above the cliffs.
There was a hackberry tree to the West.
There was a cottonwood to the East.
It flew its way between them,
North, towards a ridgeline of boulders.
Horizon to horizon, it turned and it tilted.
It feathered its wings,
Always sailing further away
Than I could ever think
The path of a leaf could go.
But then I thought,
It flew on its path,
The way we all will go.
Each leaf, each life, the wings of a bird,
Going always further than we will ever know.

A Small Ecology

Wings

Now finally, at the end,
After all these years of desert Summertimes,
Light as a feather, we feel each cool breeze,
Light as the wind of a honeybee's wings.
Now, who comes beside us here,
To brush the winged tips of our fingers?

Lost

Sparrows

From outside of the ranch house,
The sparrows come hopping hesitantly
Into the house,
In through the open door.
But when, with the slightest breath,
The door slowly closes behind them,
All the Earth they knew is changed.
And who are you and I, waiting to come one day
Into a room inside our house?
Where all that we thought to have known is gone,
And we are lost in the doorway,
In that place that we thought was our home.

GATHERING THE REMNANT

When I was the wisp of a broom
Sweeping herds of cattle
Across the great rangelands.

· · · · ·

TURQUOISE STONES IN THE CREEK BED ...
        THE SOUND OF THE HORSE'S HOOVES IN THE SAND.

A Cattle Drive

I. To Round Up the Country

When you are a cowboy gathering the country
You have to keep track of your partners.
Unless you are on the farthest sweep of a circling circle,
Or at the pivoting hub of that circle,
Or unless you only have one partner,
You will always have a partner on either side.
The working of the cattle drive will depend upon
The roughness of the country, the wildness of the cattle,
And it will depend upon how well
You are able to keep track of your partners.
Being able to know, or to predict where he or she will appear
On those furthest reaches of the horizon,
Will be very important to the success of the cattle drive.
In those shimmering distances of the desert country,
If you leave too much space between you and your partner,
You will be likely to miss a cow brute.
In rough brushy canyon country,
There is an even greater likelihood to lose cattle.
If you leave too little distance
Between you and your partner,
The drive will fail to include all the land
That the roundup foreman imagined it could.
Then another circle or another whole day's drive
Will be necessary to find most of the cattle
In a given valley, canyon, or mountain range.

How to Gather

II. What You Cannot See

Many times you will be gathering
In a rough country you've never seen before.
Your only hope is then to depend
Upon the movements of your partner.
Even at a great distance, those movements will tell you where to go.
The round-up foreman may decide to put you in the drag
Behind the cattle, to herd you and the cattle along.
But if you are experienced, he or she
May put you in a point position.
All you will need is to be able to see
The changing movements of your partner, horseback,
Riding somewhere at the edge of the shimmering distances.
You can even ride a point position in the drive
When you do not know where the herd is going.
But then, you must be very aware of your partners,
And of the herd ahead of you, and of the cattle ahead of you
That will be thrown into the herd.
If your partner goes forward in relation to the direction of the herd,
And you are on the other side of the herd
Riding a point position, you must drop back.
Then the point of the herd will come in your direction.
If your partner drops back along the side of the herd,
You need to ride forward to a stronger point position
To nudge the herd in the direction of your partner.
If you are riding a point position you will have two responsibilities.
One will be to determine the direction of the herd,
The other will be to throw the cattle you are gathering into the herd.
If you are short-handed on the drive, a point position can be a handful.
But if you whoop and whistle,
And if you are very aware of the changing needs of your partner,
Like maybe he or she could use a little help
Trying to gather a 1,500-pound Brahma bull
Who's on the prod and charging instead of being driven,

Then you will gather cattle you cannot see
Across huge valleys and mountain ranges,
Across the changing sunlight,
Across the changing rains day after day after day.

To Tell
Who You Are

Well, there's one feller around here,
Tells a lot of windy wild-cow ropin' tales.
Why, that feller couldn'a throwed his rope
Into a stock-waterin' tank,
Without gettin' his feet wet. Now, there's another one.
He don't never say nothin' about himself.
But any cowboy who partnered and rode with him
Sure had to pull his hat down mighty low,
To where he could just barely see out from under the brim,
If he was goin' to be gatherin' wild cattle with old Rex McDonald.
No sir, you don't have to tell nobody who you are. They know.

On the Roundup Trail

(To be chanted)
"White syc-a-more bark, white syc-a-more bark ...
Sun-light settin' on the syc-a-more bark ...
White syc-a-more bark, white syc-a-more bark ...
Sun-light fallin' on the syc-a-more bark ..."

Wisps of grey cloud float across the sky.
A speck of dust that drifts in the sunlight then gone.
Come on Dun-mare, let's take the creek trail for home.
Let's go, you and me ...
We'll leave this song on the trail here,
Singin' by the creek water when we're gone.

·····
A Long Day's Ride

My horse looks smaller than it did when I left.

The Ark

The Last of a Last Remnant

When cowboys are said to be gathering the remnant,
It means that nearly all the cows and calves,
Or all of the yearlings, or all of the yearling calves,
Or all of the first-calf heifers, or all of the young cows
That have missed calving twice, that you want to sell,
Or all of the bulls, or all of the bull calves,
Or all of the replacement bulls,
Or all of the steers, or all of the steer calves,
Or all of the replacement heifers,
Or all of the old cows, or all of the old bulls to be sold,
Have already been gathered.
I suppose the word "remnant" could even be applied to horses,
That is, if you had a large horse ranch,
Or maybe even to a herd of mustangs.
In any case, it means that whatever critters you are gathering,
They have all nearly been brought in,
And it means that the cowboys
Are making a last closing circle together,
To gather what is left.
But really, especially,
If you are gathering in rough country,
That is, in the mountains, or canyons, or in cedar breaks,
There will always be a lot of places
That a cowboy can't see from any great distance,
So he or she will have to ride
Nearly all the way into those places,
To know if a cow brute is hiding there.
So, in that kind of country,
There still may be a few head
That you have been unable to find,

That could be said to have been lost,
Or maybe even dead, but, somehow unaccounted for,
That is, even beyond the gathering of a last of the remnant.
And that is who I now bring to you.
While the line of cows in front of you
Slips like blood down the sandy veins in the earth,
Like water through the canyons, arroyos and draws,
And you sway back and forth across the saddle
On a sorrel horse that pushes them on
From one side of the little draw to the other,
Twisting back and forth. The cows twisting back and forth,
The horse twisting back and forth,
The cowboy's body twisting back and forth
Or you hang, head down,
By the soft shoulder hair by the horse's neck,
To get under the limbs that won't break,
Crashing, and the limbs popping off piñons and oaks,
To bring these remnant cows down through the leaves,
Out of this Sycamore Canyon.
A muley cow,
A one-horned cow,
A brown-cheeked cow ...
All dry.

To Go Up a Little Waterfall

Walter and Drum were in upper Guadalupe Canyon,
The country was very rough, almost too rough,
Even for cattle raised in Guadalupe, to make a living.
They were having trouble driving forty head of replacement heifers
Up a little waterfall towards the source of Guadalupe.
Walter was about sixty-five. Drum was thirty-two.
Walter had been raised in the canyons of the Guadalupe watershed.
They were at that place where four little canyons
Came together to spill into Guadalupe.
The lion-hunting Glenns called this area "Lion Canyon."
The homesteading Johnson family called it "Guadalupe above the Box."
The Mexicans and Drum called it *"De los Pilares por Arriba."*
Roberto called it "Salsipuedes Canyon," which meant "get out, if you can."
In that place there was an opening that could hold
About as many heifers as Walter and Drum were driving.
But the heifers would have to take the first step to go up a little waterfall,
And then higher into the basin of Lion Canyon,
From there, to the North, would be an easy drive.
Walter and Drum were sitting on their horses, at that joining place,
Waiting for one of the heifers to take the first step to go up the waterfall,
That first heifer in front of the waterfall didn't want to go,
They couldn't get close to push her, because the other heifers were in the way.
From Drum's young point of view, he felt that he and Walter had already
Waited quite awhile for the cattle to move.
So, after Drum couldn't stand to wait any longer,
He rode his horse up a ways, maybe thirty steps,
Over to where Walter was sitting on his horse, Red.
Drum asked if Walter thought, maybe, the heifers would go on up the waterfall.
"Well," said Walter, "I guess maybe they might go up the country now."
Then, he took down the coils of his saddle rope, and ran all the slack
Back through the honda, so the loop would not catch one of the heifers.
Then, as though the weight of the coils of his rope were a rock, he threw it,
Still holding to the last coil, so that he could recoil
and throw the rope again if he had to.
The coils hit her in the buttock. The heifer jumped.

She led the others up the waterfall, and higher up into Lion Canyon.
They sat on their horses for another little while,
To make sure that the hiefers could see
The easier country ahead, and also the good grass feed.
That little drive done, Walter and Drum turned their horses
To head down Guadalupe towards home.
That night at dinner, as was the custom with cowboys, they talked about the day.
Since Walter was so much older and more experienced,
With cattle and horses and rough country,
Drum asked, "How much longer would you have waited
To push all those heifers up the waterfall if I had not ridden over?"
"Well," said Walter, "When you're a-drivin' cattle through a rocky country,
And there's a real bad place that you're in, and you don't know what to do,
I've found, if you'll just wait longer than you could ever think,
That's the quickest way to go through."

Gathering the Remnant

Summer Morning

When the morning sunlight hits these blue mountaintops,
When the mockingbirds begin to call,
And the breeze blows cool down the canyon,
We'll stop here a moment to watch, on old Tico horse.
Maybe we'll hear a calf bawl,
Maybe a cow will step out from behind a bush
While these long shadows flow away into the West,
Along the mountains where the ridgelines go ...
Till that burning round ball of the sun
Lifts over the ridgeline, and it's morning.
Drum slaps the coils of his saddle rope
Against the right leg of his chaps.
"C'mon, Tico horse," he says,
"Let's go gather what's left of the remnant."

Friendship

Roberto and Drum

They are gathering the last of the remnant.
They ride by a huge blackjack oak on the canyon side.
"*Cuando viene un viento fuerte*," says Drum.
"When a strong wind comes, that old oak will fall."
"*Chingado*, damn," says Roberto.
"Some days we don't even need the wind."
Springtime and Fall, they came from prowling alone,
Tending cows along the borderline,
To gather the canyons and arroyos,
To help each other till the roundup time is done.
Now, the furthest circles had been ridden,
The yearling cattle have been shipped,
Bred cows driven to their South Winter pastures,
Again, it is time for Roberto to go.
Cada quien por su camino
Each to his own road,
Together, before the dawnlight, they saddle up.
Roberto swings his leg over the mochila,
The roll of his belongings tied behind the saddle cantle,
A handshake.
"*Hasta mañana*,"
He waves and follows the trail away into Mexico,
Across the water and wind drifts of arroyo sands.
On the rim of the Sierra Madre,
His horse slips on the rock of a shale cliff.
The horse falls from the cliff edge and rolls onto him.
And the saddle horn *se enterró*,
Buries itself in the pit of his stomach.
In that light and darkness, crossing the canyon rims,
The ringing of his spur rowels,
Echoes from the mountain rocks,
Passes across the blowing arroyo sands,
One cold hand falling from the long split reins,

"*Hasta luego,*
Que te vayas bien, hombre,
That you go well, man."
So I stay here, swaying, but still strong
With the limbs of the old oak tree,
To gather my strength at last,
And then be gone.

—*Voice of* ROBERTO

Going to Buy Heifers

The Death of Jesse Parker

We turn onto a dirt road.
Calves scamper away towards the West.
Tail hairs flying shimmering in the sunlight.
"I'll bet those little farts'll weigh five hundred pounds
In the Fall, if it rains," Bill Bryan says.
"It's been forty years since I been down this road.
Paloma my girlfriend lived right through that gap."
We stop to look towards some brindled Brahma cross cows
Come in out of the desert country to Terlingua Creek
To shade up under the cottonwoods at noontime.
"Here, by this willow spring," Bill Bryan says,
"I'll bet my granddaddy watered his horse a few times.
He's buried in that country towards the Southeast
Near Boquillas, by the Big Bend.
His grave is by the side of the new paved road.
Jesse Parker was his name.
He was cutting *guayule* on a ridge top,
When his horse came home in June.
That was the first they knew something was wrong.
It's quite a ways from here to Boquillas.
Hot as it gets in June,
By the time the horse showed up,
His body sure must have been a mess.
Bluebonnet blooming beside the road,
Yellow poppies just barely swaying,
A butterfly crossing in the morning sunlight,
Nobody knows what happened."

—Voice of BILL BRYAN

ETERNITY

Hum of the flies, the mid-morning heat,
One mourning dove calling ...
A butterfly sailing away up the canyon.
"Come on, old Macho horse,
Let's go on down off of this mountain.
We've got enough cows.
We'll head for home."

· · · · ·

TURQUOISE STONES IN THE CREEK BED ...
       THE SOUND OF THE HORSE'S HOOVES IN THE SAND.

A Blessing Way

So the Earth will bless my steps,
I walk between the juniper and the rock.
It is a hallowed place,
A grotto among the rock faces.
There I see my own, high up,
Waiting to meet me in the mountain rocks.

Eternity

Juan's Last Trail

There's old Juan, walking alone, along the ridgeline,
From Mexico Route 2, through the border fence,
Then down the rough side of the canyon to the Escondido Camp,
Where he hoped his friend, Walterio, would be waiting.
Tortillas in a sack, a half-filled bottle of tequila,
Old heart walking, centuries singing dry times,
These rangelands, and wetback trails.
His own people, Sonora, Mexico,
"Where are you headed, Juan?"
"Where there's work to do," he'd say.
Old *vaquero*, following traces of cattle trails,
Drifting through these blue Peloncillo mountain rangelands,
To find work in America.

Humming of flies, along that winding path, trembling sideoat seeds.
"*Mira*, there," says Roberto, "look past those mesquite leaves."
Faded Levi's, tan shirt, sombrero, by the cliff rock,
Where the trail climbs the ridgeline.
"Do you see him?"
A hawk goes gliding low over Juan's bones.
Sunlight and the rains, Summertime, the worms,
Odor like a cow, dead about four weeks.
Grease from his body turning the sideoats grasses brown.

Grease, coyotes, lightning, who knows?
Early Fall clouds rolling over these ridgelines,
Our bodies, clouds, dry-falling seeds,
Pretty quick a man disappears
In these winds and the creeks and the mountain sands.
Old dust in the wind, driftin' now,
On this Guadalupe Canyon trail.
Where are you headed, Juan?
"*Siempre, tengo mi camino, en la punta de los pies,*
Always, my way is before me," Juan said.
"Only the tips of my feet know where I will go."

—*Voices of* OLD JUAN *and* ROBERTO

Portrait of a Trail

Thornbush

Bachata had followed the Guadalupe Canyon trail
Nearly all of his life, to look for higher paying work
Than he could find in his homeland, to the South, in Mexico.
Now, an old man, he came a last time, up Guadalupe Canyon.
But when Drum offered him work,
He said he didn't have time. He had to go.
Drum knew he had come to say goodbye to his trail.
So now, his trail disappears in the curves of the blue distances,
In the sunlight on the rocks, in some leap of the sunlight,
Only the fires of our lives will know.

· · · · ·

Cuando yo me muera ...
When I die I will hold nothing but a handful of dust.

Passing On

Eternity

For forty years in Mexico,
He ranched in Chihuahua, Sonora, Willcox,
Empires of cattle, men and horses.
Now he's outlived his usefulness.
Now they're taking him for everything he's got.
Cheating cattle weights and contracts,
Young girls in return,
"Everybody's got to make his own mistakes,"
The old man softly says.
Eighty-two Winters worth of bent over,
Still bright, old cowboy eyes,
Walks with his hat in his hand,
Stands up when any woman comes into the room.
Still can drink anybody in the Gadsden bar under the table.
Do you know how many times he's got bucked off his horse?
How much dust he's snuffed up his nose?
How many times he's lied to the banker,
To let him hang on one more year?
"The son of a bitch is like a stone," Billy says,
"Then one day he was gone."

—*Voice of Mexico steer buyer* BILLY BROWN, *speaking of Lee Fisher*

Bone Cancer in a Cowboy Raised in Guadalupe

*Wispy blond hair, slanted smile, head cocked a little to one side as
though all the world were part comedy. Medium height, in a few more
years, he will be middle-aged.*

Monroe McPheters

"I've been a lotta places.
 I've known a lotta people.
 I've had a good life.
 I hope it don't take too long ..."

"Old Monroe was a better hand,
 Even when he was so drunk he couldn't hardly sit in the saddle,
 Than anybody else I could hire," Lee Robbins says.

"I wanted to get Monroe to ride this sorrel colt," Don Grey says.
"If you don't mind how or when I ride him, I'll do it," Monroe says.
"I may ride him down to the bar and have a beer or two,
 And leave him tied half a day and ride him home when I get through."

"If Monroe rides a colt twice a month, " Don Grey says,
"He'll do more with him than you or I could in a year."

"Me and Monroe was workin' cattle," Bud Robbins says,
"And you know, I was ridin' old Friday.
 He turns pretty good to the left with a cow,
 But he has trouble whirlin' to the right.
 I said, 'Monroe, you set on him and see what you can do.'
 The first time a cow broke to the right,
 Friday threw up his head and bloodied Monroe's lip.
 I don't know what Monroe done after that,
 But when the next cow broke to the right,
 Old Friday got down low to the ground
 Like one of them good cuttin' horses,

And bent his neck around pretty as you'd ever see.
I asked Monroe what he'd done,
And he said he thought maybe
I'd just been hurryin' Friday a little."
Two years later Drum asks,
"Monroe, what did you do to that horse?"
"If old Bud knew," Monroe says,
"He wouldn'a wanted me to ride him.
I raised my left foot up like this,
And drove that spur as hard as I could right here.
(Monroe pushes Drum high in the ribs.)
It knocked the wind out of that horse.
Old Friday just kinda went uuh ...
And got down low to the ground,
And come around with that cow.
A horse has got to make me do that.
I didn't want to do it,
but a horse that's kind of old and a little spoiled ..."

"I've had a good life.
I've been a lotta places.
I've known a lotta good people,
And a lotta good horses.
I hope it don't take too long."

ASHES

Wherever you have gone,
Wherever you will be,
In the mountains or the desert,
If you follow the arroyos, you will come to me.
There I will be, waiting for you,
Here, on this Earth, till we're done.

So I stay here, swaying but still strong,
With the limbs of the old oak trees,
To gather my strength at last,
And then be gone.

When I Am Gone

Remembering

When I am long gone away,
And the heart inside of our two bodies
Watches the Springtime flowers come,
And longs for when we were together,
When you think I am gone,
I will still be there beside you,
In the canyons of Guadalupe,
In the Cajón Bonito,
In the Animas Mountains,
The empty grass valley, the clear blue sky.
To hear the arroyos flow again,
Where we watched the first Springtime flowers come.

Springtime

When you are the bloom of the Springtime coming,
And the Fall and the Winter and the Summer are still,
When all of the force of all time comes driving
Through your heart, from those old beating veins,
Then you're no more than the flood of that old heart,
Beating, beating in the Springtime.

Oaks

Ashes

When I was young, I looked into the fire
To see what would come,
In the shapes of the glowing coals.
I rode that burning for fifty years.
Now, I look into the fire to see the old oak logs
Turn and fall into ashes.
So, it's ashes that now I'll ride,
Till the arroyos fill and the flash floods come,
To carry those light spirits away.

· · · · ·

Did you see that new moon a-comin' in, Drum?
She come in pretty wicked.
You coulda hung a powder horn from either end a' her.

Circling the Light

The Light

> While the pale ship of the quarter tipped moon
> Sails away again into the West,
> So then each wave of forever
> Comes washing around our feet.
> And because of the circling of the Earth,
> And because of the circling of the sun,
> Each dawnlit light is there for us forever.
> So we come then, into that forever,
> Again and again and again and again.

• • • • •

Turquoise Stones in the Creek Bed ...
The Sound of the Horse's Hooves in the Sand.

Glossary

Most Spanish phrases have been translated in the English text that follows them. Certain words in the cowboy and *vaquero* culture have taken on special nuances and meanings. I hope the following will clarify words to readers who are unfamiliar with that culture.

ALGERITA. A bushy plant, up to eight or nine feet tall, with small yellow berries used to make jelly.

ALMA. A woman's name. Also the word for soul.

ARROYO. A river bed, sometimes dry, sometimes flowing.

BARRANCA. Hill or slope.

BA TE RE PE. A drink traditionally made by Native Americans.

BELLOTA. White oak tree; also means acorn.

BELLOTEROS. Those who pick acorns.

BIG-BAG COW. A cow whose udder is overly filled with milk. Usually an indication that she has lost her calf.

BLUE COUNTRY. Refers to an area in East-central Arizona, probably named because of its blue color when seen in the distance.

BOOK OF MORMON. The Book of Mormon is based on divine revelation written on gold plates said to be dug from the ground by the Mormon prophet, Joseph Smith. He is said to have translated the words on the gold plates by looking through a seer's stone.

BOSAL. A *bosal* is used to control either a colt or a grown horse. Unlike a bit, which controls a horse by exerting pressure on a horse's mouth, a *bosal* only exerts pressure on a horse's nose or his cheek. It is generally made of very intricately woven rawhide.

BRONC. Usually refers to a young, untrained horse, but sometimes to an old one who has never given up his habit of bucking.

BUNCH QUITTER. A cow who doesn't want to stay with the herd. If one cowboy is driving two bunch quitters, on either side of the herd, he'll have to do a lot of extra riding.

CANTLE. The raised leather edge at the back of a Western stock saddle.

CANYON TANQUE. An impoundment of water, a pool, created with a bulldozer. Sometimes a rectangular hole called a dirt tank, it can collect water from a draw or natural source.

CATSKINNER. A man who operates a bulldozer or Caterpillar ("cat") tractor. If he is called a catskinner he probably operates it well.

CEDAR BREAKS. Rough, broken canyons in which the dominant tree is juniper, locally called cedar.

CHINGAR. This word has an English equivalent that is nearly the same as its expression in Spanish. *Chingar* means "to screw someone," as in the phrase *"Chinga tu madre, hombre."* The English would be "Oh, go screw your mother," to which the general reply is *"Y a la tuya"*–"And the same to yours, my friend."

CHIRRIONES. A tree with berries for which the line camp was named.

CLOSED REIN. A rein that is made of one piece of leather, as against a split rein, which is actually two reins.

COLD-JAWED. A cold-jawed horse does not heed the bit in his mouth.

CORRIDA. An event, a round-up.

CORRIDOS. Story songs, about an event that has occurred.

CUÑADA. Sister-in-law.

CUTTING HORSE COMPETITION. Developed from the need to separate individual animals from a herd of cattle, but cutting competitions have evolved into a highly skilled area of horsemanship. A cutter rides into the herd, splits the herd, and brings one cow to the center of the arena. Four horses and riders push that cow back towards him to show the cow-sense, skill, and agility of his cutting horse, who makes moves as violent as a rodeo bucking bronc to keep that cow from returning to her herd.

DALLY. From the Spanish *dar la vuelta*, "to take turns around" or "to give it a turn."

DICHO. A pithy saying that often reveals wisdom.

DRAW. A descending cut in the land that guides water, when there is water.

EARMARK. Ownership of rangeland cattle is determined by brand and earmark. Since brands are often difficult to read after the burnt skin has peeled and the hair has grown back, most cowboys rely on an earmark, which is a cut or a crop of an ear that can be seen at a distance to show whether a calf has been branded.

FEDERALES. The federal police of Mexico.

HACKAMORE. When young colts are first ridden, they are usually started with a hackamore instead of a bridle and bit. The nose piece of the hackamore is made of plaited rawhide, rope, or a piece of metal. The horse is directed by pressure above the nose rather than by the metal of a bit in its mouth. This allows a colt's mouth to remain tender.

HAZING. To haze along means to drive an animal, sometimes with some difficulty.

HAZING HORSE. The horse that someone rides to try to help the cowboy who is riding a bronc. In "Beto's Colt" it is arguable whether the hazing cowboy and the hazing horse, ridden by Drum, were of any help at all.

HEIFER. A heifer refers to a female, whether a calf, yearling, or young cow. As is the case with the word "filly," a young mare, the word "heifer" is sometimes applied to females of the human species.

HOBBLE. Made of rope, rawhide, or leather, a set of hobbles is usually put on the two front feet of a horse or mule to inhibit the animal's movement. Hobbles allow an animal to graze in a restricted way, but if the animal is determined, he can still travel quite a ways in a night.

HONDA. Made of rawhide, rope, or metal, and usually egg shaped, it is kind of a "keeper" that a cowboy's rope or reata slides through.

HOOLIHAN LOOP. A loop held with the palm turned up, begun on one side of the body, drawn across the chest area, at which time the hand turns over, releasing it to fall over the head of a horse or calf, which a horseback cowboy or cowboy afoot is trying to rope.

JACAL. Lean-to built of *sacahuista* or beargrass on a frame of cedar posts.

JACK MORMON. Refers to someone who may have been born into the Mormon religion but who sadly has been led astray by the stirring exigencies of the vicissitudes of a life intensely lived. (Also see Book of Mormon.)

JAVELINA. A wild boar, weighing about thirty to forty pounds. Native to the Southwest desert country of North America.

JINGLIN'. To "jingle up" means to go get a horse.

KILLDEER. A medium-sized bird found near water, whose cry sounds like the words "kill-dee, kill-dee."

LECHUGILLA. Spanish dagger, a sharp, dagger-like plant, also called *amole*.

LOFER. A wolf. Possibly comes from the Spanish word *lobo,* for wolf.

LOPE. A slow, rocking gait, a canter.

MANZANITA. A red, stiff-limbed, low-lying bush.

MAVERICK. An unbranded calf that has been weaned from its mother. With no brand, it is very difficult to know who is the true owner of the calf. Sometimes those calves are quite wild after fending for themselves without the proximity of their mother to take care of them. For this reason, Walter says, it was the custom that the maverick belonged to the cowboy who caught him.

MESCAL. An intoxicating beverage that resembles tequila, made from the mescal plant. In Mexico it is called the century plant or "agave."

MESQUITE. A thorny desert tree sometimes called "tree of the moon" in Mexico.

MOCHO. Blunt.

MOJADO. Spanish for "wet one," or the now politically incorrect "wetback," referring to Mexicans who crossed the Rio Grande to get into the U.S. *Mojar* means "to wet."

MOUNTAIN OYSTER. Refers to the cowboy practice of eating calf testicles that have been cut off and cooked on the same fire that heats the irons used to brand a calf.

MULE. The vernacular for a drug runner.

OCOTILLO. A woody plant with a red flower that can grow from one to twenty feet high, with two or three stalks (or more). Its leaves and spines that grow on the stalks are no more than an inch long.

PICKUP MEN. Two mounted cowboys who aid a bronc rider's safe dismount, after he has endured his eight-second ride.

PROWLING. Has come to mean riding through the rangeland, tending cattle with nothing specific in mind, but keeping track of the cattle, the water, the fences, and caring for what needs to be done.

PUERTA BLANCA. The Puerta Blanca (meaning "White Gate") is an old-time border crossing between Mexico and the United States, used by animals and people. It is still used, very infrequently and illegally, even today.

QUIJOTE STALK. Tall, lance-like stalk of a century or agave plant.

QUIRT. Usually a small whip made of flexible leather that rests between the second and third fingers, used to strike the horse's rump to increase his speed, or to stop him from bucking.

RAINY SEASON. In the Sonoran/ Chihuahuan Desert country there are two main rainy seasons, one in Winter and one in Summer. The Winter rains are slow and recharge aquifers and springs. The Summer rains are fierce and sudden and grow the rangeland grasses. Often they are a long time in coming.

RCA. Rodeo Cowboy Association.

REATA. A round, braided rope, woven from strands of rawhide, usually between fifty and sixty feet long, that has less wind resistance and can be thrown farther than any nylon rope. *La reata* is the source of the word "lariat."

REMUDA. Used on both sides of the border to mean the gathered mounts or horses of the *vaqueros*.

RETAQUE CORRAL. A Mexican style of corral building that forms a solid wall of sticks and limbs placed horizontally between vertical posts.

SACAHUISTA. Very bushy plant whose leaves appear as a tough clump of grass in which each leaf extends three feet.

SACKING OUT. In old-time horse-breaking, a colt is either hobbled or a back foot is tied up slightly off the ground, to inhibit the horse's movement. Then a soft gunnysack is used to drag or slap lightly over the colt. Eventually, the colt gets so used to the sack touching him all over his body that he no longer pays attention to the sack, and is then ready for a saddle to be thrown on his back. This process is call "sacking out."

SAHUARIPA. A town along the Bavispe River settled early in the nineteenth century by German families, which added a more buxom physique to the smaller Mexican population.

SIERRA MADRE. The "mother mountains," the backbone of the country, an immense range running South from Northern Mexico for a thousand miles.

SLEEPER. To sleeper a calf, a rustler ropes the calf and only cuts the ear, so the owner of the calf would think it was already branded.

STEEL DUST. In the 1970s, old-time cowboys still spoke with reverence of a line of horses that were decended from a stud horse named Steel Dust.

STOPE. An excavation resembling steps, used especially in the mining of ore.

STRADDLEJACK FENCE. A fence built over solid rock. In old times when barbwire first came to the country, it was made with wood posts forming an X near the top. Today it is made with steel posts.

VAQUERO. Cowboy (*vaca* being the Spanish word for "cow").

WINDMILL MAN. Ranch hands are often divided into two groups: those who deal with mechanical problems, and those who deal with horses or cows. Usually a man belongs to one group or the other. If a man claims he is not only a cowboy, but also a windmill man, it is a bragging statement, indicating that he can do anything.

WRANGLE. To wrangle means to bring up or herd a horse.

YEARLING. A calf that has been weaned from its mother, at approximately a year old.

Acknowledgments

To all my neighbors in the Borderlands, whose lives have touched mine to create this book; to all of my family, who have shared the journey; to my mentor, Charles Olson, and my friends Gary Snyder, Robert Creeley, Keith Wilson, Dan Morgan, and Jim Koller, who gave me the strength to complete this work; to Rebecca West, Lena Guyot, Alan Weisman, and Andrew Rush, my partners in bringing *Voice of the Borderlands* into being; and to Ilona Vukovic-Gay, for transcribing the music—my appreciation, love, and thanks.

—DRUM HADLEY

Charles Olson quotes on pages 6 and 107 come from *Call Me Ishmael: A Study of Herman Melville,* San Francisco, CA: City Lights Books, 1947. Charles Olson quote on page 328 comes from "The Kingfishers," *The Collected Poems of Charles Olson,* Berkeley, CA: University of California Press, reissued 1997.

"The Oral Tradition" (used here as a preface) first appeared in *Sonora Review* 14/15 (1988). Some of these poems previously appeared in slightly different form in *Sonora Review, Coyote's Journal,* and other literary journals, as well as in the following anthologies:

Cannon, Hal, ed. *Cowboy Poetry: A Gathering.* Layton, UT: Gibbs Smith Publishers, 1985.

Clark, LaVerne Harrell, and Mary MacArthur, eds. *The Face of Poetry.* Chico, CA: Heidelberg Graphics, 1979.

Dofflemyer, John, ed. *Maverick Western Verse.* Layton, Utah: Gibbs Smith Publishers, 1994.

Widmark, Anne Heath, ed.; foreword by Kim R. Stafford. *Between Earth and Sky: Poets of the Cowboy West.* New York: W. W. Norton & Co., 1995.

Drum Hadley's previous books include:

The Spirit by the Deep Well Tank. Santa Fe, NM: Goliard/Santa Fe, 1972.

Strands of Rawhide: Hilos de Cuero. Santa Fe, NM: Goliard/Santa Fe, 1972.

The Webbing. San Francisco, CA: Four Seasons Foundation, 1967.

Index

(Notes: names of sections and main poem heads appear in small caps; standard poem titles appear in italics; untitled poems are indexed by first line.)